EDITED BY
ANDREW RYDER,
MARIUS TABA AND
NIDHI TREHAN

ROMANI COMMUNITIES AND TRANSFORMATIVE CHANGE

A New Social Europe

T0311268

POLICY PRESS SHORTS POLICY & PRACTICE

First published in Great Britain in 2021 by

Policy Press, an imprint of
Bristol University Press
University of Bristol
1–9 Old Park Hill
Bristol
BS2 8BB
UK
t: +44 (0)117 954 5940
e: bup-info@bristol.ac.uk

Details of international sales and distribution partners are available at
policy.bristoluniversitypress.co.uk

© Bristol University Press 2021

British Library Cataloguing in Publication Data
A catalogue record for this book is available from the British Library

ISBN 978-1-4473-5750-6 paperback
ISBN 978-1-4473-5751-3 ePub
ISBN 978-1-4473-5752-0 OA ePdf

Cover design: Policy Press
Front cover image: Johanne Ryder / Romedia Foundation
Hungary
Bristol University Press and Policy Press use environmentally
responsible print partners.
Printed and bound in Great Britain by CMP, Poole

I am a Sinto, the son of a Holocaust survivor who lost six aunts and uncles in the Holocaust. I know how racism feels and I don't want anyone to endure what my people and I have to endure on a daily basis ... We not only have COVID-19 in Europe, but a pandemic that is older and even more dangerous – RACISM! Are we finally prepared to confront this reality and correct this injustice?

Romeo Franz, Member of European Parliament, Greens/EFA, speech before the European Parliament in favour of a new and more robust EU Romani policy, Brussels, 9 July 2020

A great icy mountain, an iceberg,
Is standing in front of me,
It's made out of arrogant lords ...

All of them speak of something.
All of them know something.
All of them one to another
Are telling foolish stories
        about the Roma ...

Stop it, gentleman!
Do you all want the truth?
If you want, I'll show you
Real Gypsydom *(Romanipen)*

The Roma, gentlemen
Are a people, just a people ...

Extract from Iceberg, *a poem written in 1976 by Leksa Manush (Aleksandr Belugin), a Latvian Romani poet*

Contents

List of abbreviations

BLM	Black Lives Matter
CEU	Central European University
CoE	Council of Europe
CSCE	Conference on Security and Cooperation in Europe
EC	European Commission
ERIAC	European Roma Institute for Arts and Culture
ERRC	European Roma Rights Centre
EU	European Union
FRA	Fundamental Rights Agency
GRT	Gypsies, Roma and Travellers
IRU	International Romani Union
LGBTQ	lesbian, gay, bisexual, trans and queer
LIBE	Committee on Civil Liberties, Justice and Home Affairs
NGO	non-governmental organization
NRIS	National Roma Integration Strategies
OSCE	Office of Security and Cooperation in Europe
OSF	Open Society Foundation
RC	Romani CRISS
REF	Roma Education Fund
UN	United Nations

Notes on contributors

Sarah Cemlyn, a Fellow of Corvinus University Budapest, is a long-time social practitioner, researcher and activist with Gypsies, Travellers and Roma, focusing on human rights, equality and empowerment. She undertook the first English-wide survey of social service responses to Gypsies and Travellers, led the 2009 Equalities and Human Rights Commission (EHRC) report into inequalities they experience, and participated in accommodation, education and broader policy research studies. Recently, she worked with European and British Romani women activists to analyse Romani women's and young people's activism.

Anna Daróczi holds a BA in Social Education and an MA in Gender Studies from the Central European University (CEU). She is an expert in Romani youth issues and gender equality, and worked at the Tom Lantos Institute, Hungary, managing its Romani rights and citizenship programme for two years. She has been coordinating the Voluntary Service Programme of the Phiren Amenca International Network since September 2016, where she works to empower Romani young people in civic and political participation.

Roland Ferkovics is a political scientist, researcher and advocate who focuses his professional attention on the political representation of Roma and their educational and employment inclusion in European countries. He holds an MA degree from the Department of Political Science of the CEU and a BA degree from the Department of Political Science of the University of Szeged. He currently works at the Roma Education Fund (REF) as Policy and Advocacy Officer, and, in the past, has been employed by Columbia University, CEU, Penn State University, the German Marshall Fund of the US and Morgan Stanley.

Romeo Franz is an EU lawmaker for the Group of the Greens/European Free Alliance. As a Member of European Parliament from Germany, he serves as Vice Chair of the Culture and Education Committee and is a substitute member on both the Employment and Social Affairs and the Civil Liberties, Justice and Home Affairs Committees.

James K. Galbraith holds the Lloyd M. Bentsen Jr. Chair in Government/Business Relations at the Lyndon B. Johnson School of Public Affairs and is Professor of Government at the University of Texas at Austin.

Angéla Kóczé is an assistant professor, Acting Chair of Romani Studies and Academic Director of the Roma Graduate Preparation Programme at CEU in Budapest, Hungary. During 2013–17, she was a visiting assistant professor in the Department of Sociology and Women's, Gender and Sexuality Studies Program at Wake Forest University in Winston Salem, NC, USA. She has published several peer-reviewed articles and book chapters with various international publishers, including Palgrave Macmillan, Ashgate, Routledge and CEU Press, as well as thematic policy papers related to social inclusion, gender equality, social justice and civil society.

Margareta (Magda) Matache is a justice activist and scholar from Romania, Director of the Roma Program at the FXB (François-Xavier Bagnoud) Center for Health and Human Rights, and instructor at Harvard University. In 2012, she was awarded a Hauser Postdoctoral Fellowship at the FXB Center, where she founded the university's first and only Roma Program. From 2005 to 2012, Dr Matache was the Executive Director of the Roma Centre for Social Intervention and Studies (Romani CRISS), a Roma rights organization. In 2017, she co-edited *Realizing Roma Rights* (with J. Bhabha and A. Mirga), an investigation of anti-Romani racism in Europe. Dr Matache is also the co-editor (along with J. Bhabha, C. Elkins and W. Johnson) of *Time for Reparations: Addressing State Responsibility for Collective Injustice* (University of Pennsylvania Press, forthcoming 2020).

Bernard Rorke is an Advocacy and Policy Manager for the European Roma Rights Centre (ERRC). He has worked on the rights of Roma for over two decades, and was previously Director of Roma Initiatives with the Open Society Foundation. He has a PhD in Political Theory from the Centre for the Study of Democracy, University of Westminster, UK. He is editor of *ERRC News*, Budapest correspondent for *Hope not Hate* and is a regular contributor on Romani issues.

Katalin Rostas holds a BA from the Corvinus University Budapest. She recently graduated from the Roma Access Programme of the CEU and is now a postgraduate student at the CEU in Vienna. Katalin is an activist for the rights of Roma and has worked for the Roma Education Fund as a mentor.

Andrew Ryder is a British academic and social justice campaigner based in Budapest. He is Associate Professor of Sociology at the Corvinus University Budapest, Visiting Professor at Eötvös Loránd University and a board member of the Roma Education Fund. Prior to this, he was the researcher to the All-Party Parliamentary Group for Gypsies, Roma and Travellers (based in the Westminster Parliament) and Policy Officer for the Gypsy and Traveller Law Reform Coalition (winners of the Liberty Human Rights Award in 2004). His book *Britain and Europe at a Crossroads – The Politics of Anxiety and Transformation* was published by Policy Press in 2020.

Lisa Smith joined *Travellers' Times* in October 2016 after eight years at Worcestershire's Traveller Education Service. She is currently the *Youth Traveller Times* (YTT) editor and the project manager for It's Kushti to Rokker. She has a BA in Education Studies and an MA in Inclusive Education. She is also a Global Leader for Young Children at the World Education Foundation and Chair of the Advisory Council for the Education of Romany & other Travellers (ACERT). In 2016, along with her brother Jason, Lisa produced 'Hotchi', a short drama for Channel 4.

Marek Szilvasi holds a PhD in Sociology from the University of Aberdeen, UK. He is a team manager with the Open Society Public Health Programme, and has more than ten years of professional experience in developing and implementing social justice and antidiscrimination advocacy, research, education and awareness-raising campaigns, and public litigation support strategies targeting national and international authorities across Europe. He has worked on policy change in the areas of public health, environmental justice, access to education, housing, criminal justice, migration and free movement, access to identity documents, and placement of children in care systems. Szilvasi supported development and advocated for implementation of more than 15 discrimination (national and international jurisdiction) cases. He has been a lecturer and visiting researcher at universities in Croatia, Czech Republic, Hungary, India, Italy and Slovakia.

Marius Taba has a long track record of community activism at the local and international levels. Over the last 15 years, he initiated and oversaw projects on policy development and advancement of education reforms for Roma from Central and

Eastern Europe (more than 15 countries). He was Research and Advocacy Manager at the Roma Education Fund, where he undertook applied research, grants-monitoring schemes and impact evaluation. He holds a PhD in Sociology from the University of Bucharest. He is currently a research fellow at the Corvinus University Budapest. He has held visiting lecturing posts at McDaniel College, Eötvös Loránd University and CEU, and lectures in the Romani Studies programme at the National School of Political and Administrative Studies (SNSPA), School of Governance Bucharest.

Nidhi Trehan, a political sociologist, holds a PhD from the London School of Economics and Political Science (LSE), and completed her ESRC Postdoctoral Fellowship at University College London in 2010. She is currently an Affiliated Senior Research Fellow of the CEU's Romani Studies Programme, and Fellow of the Institute of Social Sciences in New Delhi. She was a Visiting Scholar at the LBJ School of Public Affairs at the University of Texas at Austin from 2018 to 2020. Active in the areas of human rights, social policy and education as a practitioner and academic since 1996, she has published widely on the subjects of human rights and non-governmental organizations/social movements, with a focus on the Romani communities of Europe. She is co-editor (with N. Sigona) of the volume *Romani Politics in Contemporary Europe: Poverty, Ethnic Mobilization, and the Neoliberal Order* (Palgrave Macmillan, 2009) and her other publications can be found at: www.academia.edu.

Acknowledgements

We wish to thank the following for comments and feedback on some of the book chapters: Thomas Acton, Gwendolyn Albert, Sam Beck, Costel Bercus, Daniele Conversi, Will Guy, Matti Kohonen, Pierre Mirel, Carole Silverman and Violeta Zentai. We also thank the Romedia Foundation Hungary for the cover image and the Heinrich Böll Stiftung Washington, DC, for generously funding this publication.

In memoriam

During the writing of this book, two very important and inspirational Romani activists passed away: Zsuzsanna Lakatosné Danó was a well-respected community activist in Hungary; and Ronald Lee was a writer, linguist and activist for Romani civil rights in Canada. We dedicate this book to their memory and their passion for the Roma cause.

Foreword

These studies and voices from Europe's Roma lend force to the understanding that racism and exclusion are universal evils, to be fought and defeated by the common efforts of all. They provide insight into the special challenges faced by a community beset by ancient prejudice, by neoliberal austerity and now by rising ethno-nationalism in parts of Europe. They also show that in addition to these deep and dark matters, the issues faced by the Roma are not independent of the currents of social change and personal liberation sweeping across the planet.

An outsider with no special knowledge or experience can perhaps contribute little, except for an expression of solidarity and a commendation to readers that they take up these texts, read them with care and sympathy, and find in them the information, understanding and expression of what may possibly be termed 'the Romani cause'. Our task, in short, is to learn, to appreciate and to lend a hand as chance and circumstance permit.

So, having said that much, let me stand aside and let these voices, from the Romani community and its distinguished and committed friends, be heard.

James K. Galbraith
Townshend, Vermont
4 July 2020

ONE

Introduction: Romani communities in a New Social Europe

Andrew Ryder, Marius Taba and Nidhi Trehan

Cultural erasure, crisis and transformative change

This book seeks to challenge conventional discourses and analyses on deeply entrenched Romani exclusion in Europe today, which often focus narrowly on poverty and cultural identity. In this sense, our book provides new conceptual tools for framing social justice for Romani communities across Europe through the transformative vehicle of a New Social Europe. As the vast majority of Roma experience high levels of exclusion from the labour market and from social networks in society, the book maps out how the implementation of a 'Social Europe' can offer innovative solutions to these intransigent dilemmas. Finally, our work aims to serve as a policy instrument for planning and implementing new socio-economic policies on Roma in the European Union (EU).

Roma, Gypsy and Traveller communities form the largest minority ethnic group within the EU. According to the European Commission, there are an estimated 10–12 million Roma; 'Roma and Travellers' is used as an umbrella term in the definition of the Council of Europe. It encompasses Roma, Sinti, Kale, Romanichals, Boyash/Rudari, Balkan Egyptians, Eastern groups (Dom, Lom and Abdal) and groups such as Travellers, Yenish and the populations designated under the administrative term 'Gens du voyage', as well as people who identify themselves as Gypsies (FRA, 2018: 5).

The issue of identity is complex and often contentious, with some claiming the notion of 'Romani' identity presents a political agenda that is trying to fuse diverse and disparate groups into one identity to help mobilize those labelled 'Roma' in a political goal-oriented campaign that runs the danger of veering into ethnic nationalism and reflects the aspirations of a small elite. Others, though, argue that forms of common identity can be formed based on shared heritage such as language and origins, as well as shared experiences of exclusion, without creating some false and stifling cultural uniformity. Notions of a common Romani identity have been important in mobilizing and galvanizing Romani activists across Europe since the 1970s; these activists realized that given the growing prominence of the European Economic Community/EU, transnational activism would have value in European-level advocacy. Some, despairing at their national governments' inactivity, hoped to see lobbying and campaigning directed at European decision-makers prompt and prod their national governments into action to alleviate Romani exclusion (Ryder et al, 2014).

In 1993, Václav Havel, then president of the Czech Republic, described the situation of the Roma as a litmus test for Europe's civil society; yet, despite over 30 years of pan-European initiatives targeting Roma by the EU and other entities, the inclusion of European Roma remains one of the most critical challenges for European society in view of the poverty and discrimination that confronts this minority. Havel made the distinction between establishing institutions of procedural democracy and a democratic civil society, which he felt was far more of a challenge in curbing 'manifestations of intolerance even without a threat of repression' (Kamm, 1993).

At a European level, Romani peoples have been the focus of cultural erasure and grand state projects throughout history. The Hapsburgs reflected Enlightenment ideals by categorizing the Roma as a group that was outside of European culture and needed to be 'civilized' through assimilation and sedentarization. For the Nazis, the Roma, along with Jews, were classified as 'subhuman' and 'asocials', a group that needed to be eradicated through policies of genocide and the Final Solution (Friedlander, 1995). Under the communist regimes, Roma were targets of proletarianization in the belief that equality could be achieved without cultural citizenship; thus, the price to be paid was an assimilation that left little room for expressions of *Romanipe* (Szeman, 2018). Likewise, in Western Europe, commercial nomadism was proscribed in an attempt to assimilate various groups (Acton, 1974). Are current policies of 'integration' merely a benign continuation of past efforts to assimilate? Within Europe, will we continue to see policies of ethnic cleansing directed at the Roma as far-right populist politicians mesmerize the electorate with ethno-nationalist visions and authoritarian leadership?

There is an ongoing debate in the EU over how to define possible new rules and directions, and there are calls for a change in direction of EU policy vis-à-vis Roma. What direction should Europe take? What direction should be taken by institutional power? Should change also apply to Romani civil society and communities? Are non-Romani communities ready and willing to reflect on how their cultural bias and perspectives have often fuelled prejudice towards the Roma? Modernity and the rise of industrial production techniques also undermined traditional economic niches and associated ways of life enjoyed by the Roma, leading to a movement from skilled artisanal work to low-skilled, manual employment or long-term unemployment, thereby increasing the risk of assimilation and poverty. Can 'progress' and development be fair?

This Policy Short seeks to contribute to this important debate, the outcome of which will determine the political and cultural direction of European society in the early 21st century. It is a debate that is taking place in the context of acute economic, political and cultural instability in Europe, and at the time of writing, the ravages of the COVID-19 pandemic aggressively highlight the nature of Romani exclusion. We, the researchers, practitioners and activists involved in this project, are seeking to reach beyond an academic audience, and appeal to both EU and national policymakers and activists in the field. We hope this Policy Short serves as a toolkit for reflection, training and mobilization within Romani communities and among their allies. We trust our book will find appeal beyond a Romani studies readership and be viewed as a case study on how marginalized groups can achieve social justice, and will be valuable for those with a broad interest in equalities.

This book seeks to promote transformative change in society, that is, deep structural and cultural change that creates fundamental shifts in discourse and practice based on principles of social justice. It fuses personal and social development; consequently, transformative change necessitates fundamental structural, institutional, cultural and personal change, so that even at the individual level, our horizons and actions are substantially altered (Williams et al, 2010).

As Mohandas K. Gandhi (1913: 241) noted:

> We but mirror the world. All the tendencies present in the outer world are to be found in the world of our body. If we could change ourselves, the tendencies in the world would also change. As a man changes his own nature, so does the attitude of the world change towards him. This is the divine mystery supreme. A wonderful thing it is and the source of our happiness. We need not wait to see what others do.

The seeds of transformative change are within us, and it is a process that entails change from the bottom up through radical/organic social movements rooted in community organizing. Our contributors believe that new directions in activism and knowledge production, as exemplified through a new generation of Romani 'organic intellectuals' and critical thinkers, indicate that an embryonic process of transformative change has already begun within the Romani movement. We are thus critical scholars and scholar-activists challenging the status quo and seeking to fuse knowledge production with activism to promote a transformative agenda. This quest for social justice is happening in the context of crisis and flux, as well as growing intolerance and authoritarianism.

The post-war trilateral balance between the state, market and civil society has been unbalanced, with the market emerging as dominant (Foucault, 2008). The economist Thomas Piketty (2014) has highlighted how an economic elite in many advanced capitalist countries, the top '1 per cent', through the vehicle of regressive taxation policies, is returning wealth distribution backwards to levels witnessed 100 years ago, enabling them to amass huge fortunes, while working-class incomes remain stagnant. Consequently, a growing section of Europe's population is experiencing increasing hardship and insecurity, and the Roma are prominent within this category. This past decade in particular can be characterized as one of chaos and instability. What is the root and nature of this instability? A key driver is the financial crisis of 2008 as it prompted the EU and national governments to pursue austerity measures across Europe, whereby welfare budgets have been slashed and unemployment has remained high in some regions of Europe. Already at the periphery, the Roma have been among the populations suffering the greatest loss.

After the 2008 financial crisis, reports by the EU Fundamental Rights Agency (FRA) revealed the catastrophic extent of Romani exclusion. In one of the most extensive surveys on European Roma, which covered 11 EU member states, the FRA found that about 90 per cent surveyed had an income below the national poverty threshold and only about a third of those surveyed had paid work, which was often precarious and informal in nature. The FRA (2014a) also noted that in EU member states, unemployment rates for Roma were three times higher than for the general population. Romani youth are one of the most marginalized groups in society, and an estimated 63 per cent of Roma aged 16–24 were 'not in employment, education and training' (NEET). This compares to the 12 per cent EU average on the NEET rate for the same age group. Moreover, about 40 per cent of Romani children were found to live in households struggling with malnutrition or hunger (FRA, 2014a). The FRA (2014a) also found that, despite discrimination, most Roma were actively seeking work, contrary to the widespread racist trope of indolence. Moreover, only 12 per cent of the Roma aged 18 to 24 who were surveyed had completed upper-secondary general or vocational education, compared with over 70 per cent of the majority population (FRA, 2014b). In addition, exclusion has an important gender dimension: while 14 per cent of Romani men said that they had never been to school, the percentage for Romani women was 19 per cent. In its survey, the FRA (2014c) found that across EU member states, only 21 per cent of Romani women were in paid formal work, compared to 35 per cent of Romani men.

Progress has been limited in reducing avoidable and unnecessary health inequalities endured by Romani people, and they continue to die young. Disproportionately burdened by chronic but preventable diseases, often omitted from prevention programmes and marginalized within healthcare systems, their life expectancy and health status remain significantly lower than for their non-Romani counterparts in all European countries (EPHA, 2018). In the wake of the 2008 financial crisis, negligible progress has been made in achieving social justice for the Roma. A safe water supply and sanitation services are available to almost every non-Romani household in Europe today; yet, many Romani populations cannot access these essential services and lack clean tap water, flushing toilets and hot showers. Such exclusion is, in part, not just a product of poverty, but also attributable to spatial exclusion and environmental racism that leads to large numbers of Roma being consigned to segregated ghetto communities where slum housing lacking basic utilities occupies marginal space.

Critically, current socio-economic problems for Roma and others at the margins run deeper than the financial crisis. Since the collapse of communism, countries in Central-Eastern Europe have been propelled on a trajectory of neoliberalism as they joined the EU, leading to the promotion of laissez-faire economics, which has discouraged and limited state intervention and moved away from the original conception of the European social model. As state enterprises were privatized or closed down, large numbers of Roma working as manual or semi-skilled workers were made redundant. In some 'left behind' communities, Romani families have not had a stable and reliable income for three decades. In Western Europe, the growing dominance of neoliberal policies, bolstered by the EU's promotion of a single market, has also made the economic livelihoods of many more precarious through privatization and structural decline, and Roma have borne the brunt of these consequences. Despite the huge social costs of neoliberalism, as reflected in the case of the Roma, it has bolstered its position through forms of divide and rule, most notably, by depicting the marginalized and unemployed as lazy and work-shy. Such pathologizing through a 'culture of poverty' narrative thus views exclusion as something that is inherited and to which people are socialized into (rather than structurally rooted), and has a strong racialized dimension. This interpretation of poverty is, at times, coupled with racist narratives, whereby ethnic groups such as the Roma, alongside migrants, are demonized in the public sphere as prone to criminality and welfarism.

Nationalism is the dominant ideology of the modern age, being based on a notion of popular sovereignty that sees the people as coterminous with the nation and as a bounded and congruent entity (Conversi, 2007). The Roma are often viewed as outside the boundary of 'insiders', a hostile perception orchestrated against them by the media and political class. The impact of nationalism has been accentuated by economic crisis and cultural change, making national identity appear to be a safe haven and a reassurance of 'traditional' certainties in an age of acute anxiety. The instability of nationalism and ability to morph into extremes is evident with the rise of its shrill offshoot: authoritarian populism. Authoritarian populism has encouraged a form of 'emergency politics' where often charismatic and 'strong' personalities, largely men, offer simplistic analyses and solutions to the ills of the world, centred on attacks on liberal democracy and multiculturalism, and usually involving scapegoating minority groups, who become 'folk devils' (Cohen, 1972). Such narratives also rely on a reified form of national identity that is static, insular and narrow, and defines itself through the classification of 'outsider' groups, often centred on vulnerable minorities like the Roma (Mudde and Kaltwasser, 2017). Romani communities, already racialized, are now being increasingly securitized, whereby they are perceived as a risk and danger to society, with accusations of anti-social behaviour, welfare dependency and spatial encroachment through nomadism and or migration (van Baar et al, 2019). Such accusations are evident in the media and authoritarian populist rhetoric, which is increasingly 'tabloidized' and emotive. In a 'post-truth' age, scant attention is given to balance and accuracy; instead, emotion and accusation appears to be at a premium in the public sphere, the arena of public debate. The rise of social media has also contributed to the demonization of Roma.

Europe appears to be on the verge of a precipice in terms of political instability. Robert Fico's government in Slovakia has been linked to the mafia, ties that led to the murder of an investigative journalist probing corruption. In Hungary, Viktor Orbán revels in challenging the tenets of liberal democracy and, alongside the political leadership of Poland, is challenging many of the fundamental principles of the EU. In Italy, Matteo

Salvini, controversial radical-right politician and former interior minister, hopes to return to power. Across Europe, radical-right and nationalist parties wait in the wings, hoping to attain power, and could seek to emulate Britain's exit from the EU (Brexit), a huge challenge to the EU. Steve Bannon, a former adviser to President Donald Trump, established a pan-European populist umbrella group, 'The Movement', which worked for populist gains being made in the EU elections in 2019; although this did not materialize, there remains the possibility that future economic crises could tip the balance in their favour.

The rise of authoritarian populism in Europe has parallels with political developments in the US under President Trump. This book contains in-depth discussion of authoritarian populism in Hungary under Orbán and its impact on Roma, believing that it is an outlier for future developments in Europe, but also devotes itself to looking at what lessons the Romani social movement and wider campaigns for social justice in the US and Europe might learn from each other, with reference to a counter-narrative of resistance. The rise of authoritarian populism could reflect the warnings issued by two great thinkers of the 20th century, Karl Polanyi and Ralph Dahrendorf, who foresaw that capitalism – when in deep crisis – might transform into forms of fascism and authoritarianism (Ryder, 2020). These new detours of neoliberalism initially appear to be in contradiction with globalization, as reflected by sentiments favouring a retreat into the nation-state and opposition to free movement of labour, but the fusion of neoliberalism and authoritarian nationalist populism seems to be a relatively simple form of political merger, facilitating the further downsizing and dilution of social protections (Fekete, 2016). Such a development will have profound implications for the Roma.

COVID-19 – a pandemic coronavirus that has already killed large numbers of people across the world – brutally exposes the fragility and precarity of life for many at the margins, including the Roma. COVID-19 has exacerbated Romani marginalization, with lockdowns that have left Roma, especially those dependent on informal and casual work, without an income, bank account or access to savings, and with little or no emergency welfare support coming from the state. A poor health profile and high levels of diabetes and other debilitating pre-existing conditions, together with overcrowded substandard living conditions in rural settlements and tenement housing, leave many Roma vulnerable to the virus. Moral panics and hysteria in countries such as Spain, Bulgaria, Romania and Slovakia have centred on Romani communities, with claims that they are the principal carriers of the virus. For instance, in Bulgaria, some politicians and media outlets referred to Romani people as 'a threat to public health' and requested special measures targeting them on that basis. Local authorities in several EU member states have set up draconian police checkpoints around Romani settlements to enforce quarantine measures; in one place, a fence was erected around a Romani settlement to better control movement (CoE, 2020). Such actions were redolent of earlier (often recurring) anti-Romani racist measures in Europe generated by moral panics. For example, during the time of Romani slavery in Romania, enslaved nomadic Roma were forbidden from entering the city of Bucharest during outbreaks of the plague. Then, in the 1940s, fears that Roma would contaminate the 'Romanian race' with typhus led to stringent anti-Romani measures (Matache and Bhabha, 2020). The COVID-19 pandemic has triggered a major economic collapse that may well last several years, and the Roma have been adversely affected by this slump. Thus, communities already on the margins will be devastated as first the pandemic and then economic precarity take their grim toll. Only the resilience of grass-roots organizers and the leadership and resourcefulness of authorities (such as local mayors) could act as bulwarks against the immediate instability (Dunai, 2020).

Policy and activism

Shortly after the advent of the financial crisis, in 2011, the EU initiated a new policy framework for the Roma, the National Roma Integration Strategy (NRIS), which is critically assessed in Chapter One; however, as is evident from the FRA evaluations cited earlier, its progress has been slow and some would say negligible. The European Roma Rights Centre (2016: 1) concluded:

> Five years on, the EU Framework has hit 'a mid-life crisis'. Nearly one decade after the launch of this initiative, it can be said that the EU Framework for National Roma Integration Strategies has yet to deliver in terms of concrete change to the lives of millions of Europe's Romani citizens; the implementation gap is more pronounced than ever; discrimination and segregation remain pervasive and human rights abuses against Roma are all too frequent.

In the post-war period, development theory was dominant and contended that through planning and intervention, deprived groups located at the margins of society could be assisted in benefitting from forms of mainstream existence premised on Western capitalist notions. This was subsequently denounced by post-development theorists, who argued that development theory implied a form of control through the concept of 'governmentality', which normalized a neoliberal and assimilative policy agenda and 'responsibilization', thus individualizing the victims rather than addressing the structural fault lines on the ground. These traits have been evident with reference to programmes focused on the Roma (van Baar, 2011). As noted in this book, Romani civil society has too often been disconnected from the communities it seeks to represent and/or tied to, as well as restricted by donor-led agendas, which have in some cases made civil society organizations service providers and adjuncts of institutional power (Trehan, 2001).

One encouraging development within Romani activism has been the emergence of forms of transnational activism. In 1971, for example, the International Romani Union (IRU) was formed, creating a global umbrella group for the diverse Romani diaspora, which strengthened networks within Europe, that is, between the eastern and western halves, as well as with Roma in the USSR and the Americas. Regrettably, such initiatives are often undermined through factionalism as an organizational culture characterized by a traditional/patriarchal leadership often seeks to monopolize power and obstruct innovation, most notably, with the voices of Romani women and youth going unheard. In some cases, deeply nationalistic frames preclude the development of solidarity, intersectional alliances, friendship and cooperation, with other groups experiencing exclusion (Klimova-Alexander, 2005).

Since the collapse of communist one-party rule in Eastern Europe, a number of international Romani non-governmental organizations (NGOs) have emerged, largely dependent on the Hungarian-American billionaire philanthropist George Soros's Open Society Foundation. Nonetheless, some scholars and activists argue that such entities have failed to create a dynamic and sustainable social movement with strong links to communities at the margins. A new generation of Romani leaders – often university-educated and fluent in English – are to be found in such NGOs but critics say they are disconnected from communities at the grass roots and are often restrained by corporate-style management structures within civil society (Gheorghe, 2013). Others argue that Romani civil society has too often fallen into a narrow 'liberal civil rights' frame focused on a human rights and liberal multiculturalism discourse that neglects the economic dimension of Romani exclusion and fails to offer a narrative that challenges the neoliberal order (Trehan, 2009). Despite all these criticisms, it is important to reflect on where the Roma would be without this work having been done, and some suggest that it has laid invaluable foundations for future empowerment, producing a cadre of educated leaders able to engage in strategic policy development. Another cause of optimism is that a new, critically minded cadre of Romani activists are coming to the fore; despite the scale of new challenges and crisis, opportunities are presenting themselves to advance transformative change.

While identity politics under the banner of Romani activism should avoid static and homogenizing conceptions of identity, it is a 'label' that can assist in the 'strategic essentialism' of Spivak, namely, mobilizing identity to form communities of fraternity and performances of identity to achieve recognition and/or access to resources (Landry and MacLean, 1996). While not imposing rigid uniformity, it is a concept that entails essentialization of identity but, equally, promotes discussion and dialogue around shared ideals that should be reworked and updated. Spivak later expressed doubts about the term but it has been influential in the development of feminist, queer and postcolonial theory. It is a useful concept in describing the mobilization of 'Roma' since the 1970s, a galvanization some fear may, at times, have led to the overt promotion of nationalist and culturalist agendas among Romani activists (Surdu and Kovats, 2015).

However, we believe the contours of the new Romani EU policy and Romani social movement should encompass *both recognition and redistribution* in a meaningful sense. While it is true that the EU and Romani civil society have embraced the frames of 'recognition and distribution' to some degree, the EU NRIS framework stresses the importance of social and ethnic inclusion. Despite these efforts, recognition has been undermined by tokenistic measures and representation, as well as the wider societal securitization and demonization of Roma, while a shallow form of redistribution has centred on a narrow social inclusion agenda centred primarily on training and skills development that works in tandem with the tenets of neoliberalism (Van Baar and Vermeersch, 2017). We believe the concept of a New Social Europe offers opportunities to bring to the fore meaningful conceptions of recognition and redistribution, as well as innovative directions in Romani advocacy and community organizing.

A New Social Europe

Although rarely discussed today, 'Social Europe' was a visionary concept in the 1970s and 1980s, promoted by social-democratic/left voices in Western Europe who sought to achieve democratic socialism in Europe via the European Economic Community (now EU). According to Andry (2017), the concept of Social Europe centred on: wealth redistribution; social and economic planning; economic democratization; improved working and living conditions; regulation and control of economic forces; guarantee of the right to work; upward harmonization of European social regimes; and access to social protection for all. Furthermore, it included environmental concerns and sought the democratization of the European Community's institutions, to empower the European Community in the social field and greater social and economic coordination between member states. For some, it was a civilizational project based on Enlightenment values promoting forms of solidarity and cosmopolitanism.

The nearest this project came to realization was the EU Commission under its President Jacques Delors (1985–95). Under his leadership, the Social Charter was introduced, guaranteeing fundamental social and economic rights as a counterpart to the European Convention on Human Rights, which concentrates on civil and political rights. It guarantees a broad range of everyday human rights related to employment, housing, health, education, social protection and welfare. Nonetheless, Delors found his nemesis in British Prime Minister Margaret Thatcher, who bitterly opposed the Social Charter, disparaging it as 'socialism through the back door', a corporatist form of socialism that would undermine the neoliberal deregulatory form of government she had pioneered (Turner, 2000).

It was the ascendancy of neoliberalism that constrained and undermined the impetus for a Social Europe, and the European Commission increasingly reflected the aspirations and political mores of Europe's conservative centre, according greater priority to the economic agenda of strengthening the single market and free trade, rather than the social dimension of the EU. Simultaneously, the mainstream Left in Europe lost its confidence and resolve in the face of the neoliberal paradigm shift, and developed what became known as the 'Third Way', a diluted form of left politics that embraced the tenets of neoliberalism within a framework of limited and modest social policy, best exemplified by New Labour (Levitas, 2005). As such, the European Left lost its will and inclination to radically reform and reorient the European project on the basis of socialist principles. Now, of course, the European project itself has come under attack from forms of authoritarianism/ national populism (discussed earlier) and the more aggressive forms of neoliberalism espoused by the US and UK that are even more deregulatory, as well as opposed to supranational initiatives that while committed to free trade, also pledge to protect social rights and defy a 'race to the bottom'.

In December 2019, a former minister in German Chancellor Angela Merkel's cabinet, Ursula von der Leyen, became the latest President of the European Commission. Despite the political, economic and cultural challenges outlined earlier, there seems to be little evidence of new initiatives that might create a fairer and more dynamic EU for those at the margins like European Roma. French President Emmanuel Macron has called for a 'rebuilding' centred on an integrated Eurozone with its own finance minister, parliament and a stand-alone budget to head off future crises. However, we argue that a lack of critical reflection on the inherent weaknesses of neoliberalism – a hollowing out of the state and concomitant public services, increasing inequality, and often an erosion of democratic norms that leads to oligarchic power – as well as the bureaucratic dimension Macron envisages, may not be the most effective remedy; rather, his centrist 'Third Way-like' approach is unable to meet the full range of authoritarian populist challenges facing Europe.

The founders of the EU project envisaged diverse forms of economic and social solidarity safeguarding the European social model (Crouch, 2017). This book sheds light on how the EU can be reinvented and energized through a 'New Social Europe' that takes active measures to include Europe's largest and youngest demographic, the Romani communities. To this end, we explore how the concept of Social Europe can offer a pathway towards achieving social and economic justice for Romani communities. We are thus critical scholars and activists challenging the status quo and seeking to fuse knowledge production with community mobilization in order to promote a transformative agenda centred around anti-racism and economic justice as pillars of the New Social Europe vis-a-vis Romani communities.

'Social Europe' today stresses the value of increasing labour market participation through active welfare state measures, emphasizes supply-side efforts at job creation, seeks measures to provide security other than lifetime job tenure and prioritizes efforts to combat social exclusion (Seikel, 2016). The Democracy in Europe Movement 2025 (DiEM25) is a pan-European movement which believes that the EU is disintegrating, as reflected in misanthropy, xenophobia and toxic nationalism, but wishes to promote solidarity in the EU through a European New Deal that 'primes the pump', injects state finance into the economy, stimulates economic activity and creates jobs and opportunities for all. It is also a movement that countenances ecological balance and a fossil fuel-free world; hence, regeneration and economic stimulus and growth should be based on sustainability, entailing new forms of production and work, including shorter working weeks and the redistribution of working hours. This would also mean curbing the current excesses of consumerism and materialism.

Wilkinson and Pickett's (2009) *The Spirit Level: Why More Equal Societies Almost Always Do Better* is relevant to our analysis of the profound multidimensional inequality facing the Roma. They posit that redistribution and fairer societies benefit all: work and fairer societies reduce the cost and trauma of inequality, creating social and political stability. In this book, we highlight how greater inclusivity will benefit Roma and non-Roma alike. More broadly, in terms of how we manage our resources and economies, progressives are advocating the democratization of institutions like the International Monetary Fund and World Bank, as well as the possibility of a reconstituted global governance structure as a means to make a fairer and more equitable world that moves away from the market fundamentalism of the 'Washington Consensus' (Jones and O'Donnell, 2018). We support such a reorientation.

While the debate in recent decades on Romani inclusion has centred on human rights, critics argue that a neoliberal human rights agenda only allows for tokenistic concessions, leaving the fundamental nature of society unchanged (Trehan, 2009; Law and Kovats, 2018). This view certainly has validity as the Roma have experienced little material improvement in their situation, despite being protected by human rights norms (even stronger within the EU), and targeted by initiatives by human rights agencies and NGOs. However, such criticism may be is too harsh. Where would the Roma be today without human rights protections? Perhaps it is a problem of the interpretation and application of human rights. A more radical definition of human rights would entail perceiving poverty as multidimensional and seeking to challenge it by inviting analysis of the structural causes of poverty (such as anti-Romani racism), as well as tackling its symptoms. Lister (2004) argues that laying claim to legal entitlements has symbolic rhetorical force, enabling a re-conceptualization of poverty that moves away from personal shame. Such a radical conception of human rights identifies a dual politics of redistribution and of recognition and respect since the entitlements encompass both socio-economic rights and citizenship rights (for example, the right to participate fully in society irrespective of ethnicity and the concept of 'cultural citizenship') (Szeman, 2018). Thus, the predicament of Romani communities is reframed, and support is no longer seen as charity, but instead becomes a duty. Furthermore, instead of being bounded by xenophobic tropes labelling them as 'indolent' and 'welfare-dependent', the Roma at the margins would be perceived as victims of an unfair system deserving of social (and economic) justice, necessitating structural change (compare Chapter Two by Ferkovics et al on EU policy with Chapter Seven by Trehan and Matache on anti-racist analysis). Such a narrative has transformative potential in a New Social Europe, and offers a critical challenge to economic hegemony, explaining, in part, why the radical right has sought to defy and undermine even liberal forms of human rights today.

A radical human rights discourse committed to challenging multidimensional poverty and exclusion is the hallmark of economist Amartya Sen's 'capabilities approach', promoting an individual's capability to achieve the kind of life they have reason to value. Such an approach seeks to dismantle multifaceted barriers to inclusion, including not only poverty and access and rights to resources, but also freedom of expression and identity, and the ability to participate in decision-making and to be heard. It facilitates the capability to make valued choices and is thus not prescriptive. It is therefore of relevance to the Roma in the sense that it avoids previous forms of assimilation and allows paths of inclusion to be framed that reflect the cultural, social, economic and moral aspirations of those at the margins. As such, it prioritizes agency, and this is another central theme of this book.

In the past, conceptions of Social Europe have been too statist and given little thought to the agency and self-empowerment of oppressed groups. This book envisions a New Social Europe that promotes forms of community action that can facilitate bottom-up, inclusive community development, which focuses on harnessing the existing resources and skills of those at the margins. This also means employing customs and traditions as resources that can be adapted and built upon rather than discarded (asset-based community development). We argue that a vibrant and autonomous civil society for not just Roma, but all minority groups and interests, is a prerequisite to ensuring that macro-policies are relevant to and shaped and led by local communities, and that platforms are provided to challenge oppressive forms of ideology and practice.

Here, Sen's capabilities approach has relevance, and in this volume, we seek to demonstrate how change – not just in material conditions and access to services, but also in empowerment and a broad range of opportunities and possibilities – can create tailored and relevant solutions to particular Romani communities' needs, rather than the prescriptive and top-down blanket approaches of the past. However, the reality is that many NGOs are not sustainable at present given that they have become extensions of the neoliberal project and/or are engaged in work that the state should actually be providing but, due to the prevalence of neoliberal policies, has abdicated/forgone (education, healthcare, legal aid and so on). The current NGO map has few real community service organizations (CSOs) that serve local Romani communities and that privilege people-centred priorities. We argue a vibrant democracy should provide for the ability of members of civil society to organize and represent community interests, and have the resources to enable financial autonomy and unbridled challenges to power. This may come about through greater governmental financial support but with less prescription, through civil society becoming more self-financed, through genuine co-production or through a combination of all three.

Critics of the strategies of the contemporary Romani movement contend that an emphasis on narrow identity politics has meant liberal reformist and cultural aims have taken precedence over structural change (Law and Kovats, 2018). This reflects the tension Fraser (1995) recognized between redistribution and recognition, where demands for 'recognition of difference' have fuelled struggles of groups mobilized under the banners of nationality, ethnicity, 'race', gender and sexuality. In such 'post-socialist' conflicts, group identity has supplanted class interest as the chief medium of political mobilization. Cultural domination supported by nativist ethno-nationalist claims and exclusionary policies supplants conventional forms of exploitation as the fundamental injustice, and cultural recognition has displaced socio-economic redistribution as the remedy for injustice and the goal of political struggle. In recognizing the interrelation between economy and culture, however, Fraser (2007) notes that solutions and viable strategies take a multitude of forms. Like Fraser, we privilege transformative action that is fundamental and structural above that which is reformist and affirmative; however, we do acknowledge that important change can stem from the latter, which can even evolve into something that becomes transformative. Hence, purist disputes over hierarchies of resistance that revolve around a debate contrasted between recognition and redistribution do not need to be so binary or polarizing. While we argue that recognition and redistribution can be fused, the prevailing current of public opinion appears to be moving against such sentiments. In an age of economic crisis and cultural dislocation where tradition and convention have been challenged through globalization, many have retreated into the certainties of rigid forms of national identity and chauvinism.

The sociologist Anthony Giddens (2014) has stated that the world is increasingly being divided between forms of economic, political and/or religious fundamentalism and cosmopolitanism. Liberal multiculturalism sought to eradicate racism through education and law, and is now increasingly derided. Some political elites are not only stressing the need for integration, but also actively orchestrating forms of nativism (which often leads to state-sponsored racism). The book assesses the relevance of the term 'antigypsyism' (a perception that a particular form of racism is directed at the Roma) in the context of the points Giddens raises and the cultural war that European society appears to be increasingly engaged in, where society is fractured and polarized along the lines of values, beliefs and practices. This cultural war has a demographic dimension as well, where older, less educated and rural sections of the population are pitted against the young, diverse and metropolitan. For some, the answer to these tensions rests in colour-blind policies centred on universal conceptions of citizenship (Kovats and Law, 2018). For others, targeting and ethnic-based policies offer tailored policy responses and platforms for community voices (Cortés, 2019). Still others believe that inclusive notions of national and European citizenship can offer universality while not precluding forms of targeting, which should be viewed as forms of piloting and emergency measures that can be absorbed into the mainstream of a New Social Europe centred on intervention and redistribution that can ultimately address many of the underlying socio-economic tensions and anxieties that fuel the 'culture war' (Ryder and Taba, 2018). Critical Romani voices also contend that intersectionality, solidarity with other marginalized groups and privileging the knowledge derived from lived experiences of poverty, racism, spatial exclusion, sexism and so on can serve to counter the reactive narratives spawned by the culture war, and should be part of the narrative of a New Social Europe.

Critical Romani voices are also evident in this book through critical race theory, which contends that racial inequality emerges from the social, economic and legal differences created between dominant and hegemonic 'races' to maintain elite privileges in labour markets and politics, and consequently create the circumstances that give rise to marginalization. Postcolonial thought also informs this book, and is described as an attempt by those once subject to colonialism to break free from rigid doctrines of Eurocentrism and elite nationalism, and to aspire to give a standpoint and voice to the (collective) underprivileged subjects of the Global South, who were often silenced and/or misrepresented by the very same elite European discourses. Here, a first parallel can be drawn with Roma, who have similarly been deprived of voice, agency and history in European narratives. Spivak (2017) asked the question of whether the subaltern (those at the margins) can speak for themselves as cultural repression and marginalization limits such scope. It is therefore pertinent to ask 'Who speaks for the Roma?' and 'How can agency and voice be enhanced for the Roma?' (Trehan and Kóczé, 2009; Ryder and Szilvasi, 2017).

In 2020, there was a glimmer of hope for a New Social Europe. In July 2020, an EU summit was held to finalize the details of an economic rescue package to prevent what appeared to be the worst economic crisis since the great depression of the 1930s, a threat that loomed large as a consequence of the COVID-19 pandemic. Divisions were evident between member states with a conservative economic tradition of being opposed to securing credit for economic stimulus, those termed 'frugals', as opposed to those states more willing to used credit during economic crisis to 'prime the pump', re-start the economy, who can be termed as 'the primers' (Saxer, 2020). The finalised deal involves €750 billion package and involves significant financial transfers from the richest countries to the weakest. For the first time, the European Commission will be allowed to borrow large sums on the international money markets. This fundamentally changes the scope of the organization. No longer will it depend entirely on funds transferred from member states.

What is also significant is that Germany, normally allied with the 'frugals', backed the 'primers'.

Varoufakis (2020), the former Greek Finance Minister, was sceptical as in his opinion the recovery fund is a distraction from the elephant in the room: massive austerity. Furthermore, he was not convinced that Germany has been persuaded to drop its ordoliberal commitment to balanced books, and in his opinion, the proposed fund is 'minuscule', insufficient to deal with the impending economic tsunami. Time will tell whether the rescue package is effective and if there has been a paradigm shift in Europe. The contributors to this book support this shift and hope the ideas presented here can shape high level policy discussions with reference to the Roma.

To reiterate, our vision of a New Social Europe is based on redistribution and intervention as central tools in achieving social justice. We wish to see forms of development that nurture both growth and agency that are not set within neoliberal frameworks centred on profitability and forms of governmentality. A New Social Europe embodies not only social justice, but also freedom and agency, ideas that in recent decades the radical right has sought to make its own through laissez-faire deregulatory conceptions of what it is to be free (Varoufakis, 2019). Within a New Social Europe, the social contract is strengthened as people are provided sufficient resources by the state to enable and enhance their capabilities and access decent life chances, including Romani communities at the margins. A New Social Europe gives people the freedom to express identities and nurtures solidarity and an intersectional dialogue that deconstructs and challenges both cultural and economic hegemony. A New Social Europe gives people the freedom to understand and discuss through a revived public sphere, where a well-resourced civil society connected to the grass roots provides platforms, agency and critique. This is how we envision transformative change. Given the critical challenges Europe faces with COVID-19, a new economic crisis and a widening social gap for groups like the Roma, the concept and transformative vision of Social Europe has never been more relevant.

To recap, the book addresses a series of key questions:

- What should a New Social Europe mean? How can transformative change be achieved?
- What role can the EU, member states, civil society and the academy play in creating a New Social Europe?
- How can recognition and redistribution be achieved?
- How can we halt the corrosive spread of anti-Romani racism and authoritarian nationalism?
- How can Romani communities achieve agency and self-empowerment?
- How can we unite diverse marginalized groups using intersectional approaches within a New Social Europe? How can the voices of Romani women and others experiencing patriarchy and oppression be heard?
- What lessons can Europe and the US draw from each other in terms of resistance to authoritarian populism?

Outline of the book

Having set out the conceptual framework in this introductory chapter, the book proceeds as follows:

- In Chapter Two, Roland Ferkovics, Andrew Ryder and Marek Szilvasi propose a dynamic EU social policy encompassing redistributive and interventionist policies, coupled with bolder forms of empowerment.
- In Chapter Three, Marius Taba identifies how authoritarianism and nationalist populism are working against the Roma through 'antigypsyism', and outlines the potential for intersectional solidarity and transformative change.
- In Chapter Four, Bernard Rorke provides insights into how the authoritarian populist Prime Minister of Hungary, Viktor

Orbán, is stirring anti-Romani sentiments and stoking hatred to bolster his power.

- In Chapter Five, key Hungarian Romani activist Jenő Setét is interviewed by Katalin Rostas.
- In Chapter Six, Anna Daróczi, Lisa Smith and Sarah Cemlyn provide important insights into the perceptions of Romani youth on Social Europe, transformative change and intersectionality.
- In Chapter Seven, Nidhi Trehan and Margareta Matache examine the experiences of transatlantic Romani activists and the implications for an inclusive political agenda and policy for Romani communities based on the concepts anti-racism, community organizing and solidarity.
- In Chapter Eight, Angéla Kóczé and Nidhi Trehan offer a critical theoretical contribution to re-imagine and re-envision Social Europe by using the language and insights of Romani feminists who challenge the norms of intersected gendered, racial and classed violence, not as accidental, but rather as systemic conditions of neoliberal capitalism.

The volume concludes in an Afterword with reflections by German Greens MEP Romeo Franz.

The Romani 'ideas tree' for transformative change

Some of the ideas raised in this Policy Press Short were discussed at a conference staged in Budapest in 2018 and hosted by the Corvinus University, European Roma Rights Centre and Roma Education Fund, among others. The conference, 'The Roma and Social Europe', was attended by Romani community members, activists, service providers and researchers. The discussion was crystallized into what we describe as the 'The Romani ideas tree for transformative change'. This is not so much a manifesto, but rather a guide and catalyst for communication, debate and strategic activism. As with a tree, we hope it will be added to, nurtured and developed, and grow deep roots and maintain an organic connection to the base (of Romani communities). The 'ideas tree' has shaped and guided much of the discussion in the book.

Within a New Social Europe, we wish to see the following in society:

1. New economic systems should be created that promote redistribution and intervention, and recognize the social and economic failure of the current economic system, securing levels of employment and support for entrepreneurialism, mutualism and social enterprise, welfare, and skills development sufficient to create a just society. In this sense, the conception of a renewed Social Europe has relevance if coupled with policies that promote and celebrate diversity and inclusivity.

2. In a changing global economy, the collectively available workload of a society should be more equally divided, creating universal basic employment in which (lifelong) learning is considered to be an integrated part of employment.

3. An education system should exist that is free and not segregated, that translates and ingrains concepts of diversity, tolerance and respect, and that does not indoctrinate nationalism and other ideas that define Roma and other minority groups as separate and inferior. Such an educational system would not only recognize that equality is important, but also acknowledge that positive measures need to be in place to close outcome gaps and achieve equity.

4. Roma civil society should be a key partner in decision-making and able to build organizations that are democratic and have the capacity to mobilize communities at the grass roots. This may necessitate greater self-funding, or donor funding that is more flexible and sympathetic to localized NGOs and activism.

5. While a new generation of Roma lawmakers, activists, researchers and artists are now taking the political

and cultural stage, many Roma at the margins should be empowered.

6. More interaction between rural, grass-roots Roma NGOs and activists and those in urban centres should be encouraged. This could be achieved through the generation of new mechanisms of knowledge production, communication and solidarity, so that both urban and rural communities are enriched.

7. The diversity and fluidity of Romani communities, both culturally and along dimensions of gender, class and sexuality, should be recognized as a major strength in generating new insights, energies and intersectional solidarity. This recognition may also cause some creative disruption to existing dominant patterns and modes of organizing among Romani communities.

8. Romani culture should be celebrated in societies where diversity and interculturalism are promoted, and where knowledge production in the community as well as the academy is considered to have merit.

9. Democracy and free speech should be safeguarded against authoritarianism and nationalist chauvinism, which are major instigators of forms of antigypsyism, hate speech and crime. Positive political narratives both within and outside of the communities need to be developed and used. The narrative should be potential-based, emphasizing the capacities of Roma in a social, political and economic sense. Furthermore, the narrative should point out the common points between Romani and non-Romani communities, bridging the interest of the two. Additionally, the narratives need to reflect on the very fact that challenges that Roma face are not solely an ethnic phenomenon, but rather affect the entire population, requiring coordinated joint work for the common good cause.

10. The EU and member states should champion these values and devise a new bolder Romani strategy, with clearer

targets and interventions, working collaboratively with Romani communities.

References

Acton, T. (1974) *Gypsy Politics and Social Change*, London: Routledge.

Andry, A. (2017) '"Social Europe" in the long 1970s: the story of a defeat', PhD thesis, European University Institute.

CoE (Council of Europe) (2020) 'Governments must ensure equal protection and care for Roma and Travellers during the COVID-19 crisis', www.coe.int/en/web/commissioner/-/governments-must-ensure-equal-protection-and-care-for-roma-and-travellers-during-the-covid-19-crisis

Cohen, S. (1972) *Folk Devils and Moral Panics: The Creation of the Mods and Rockers*, London: MacGibbon & Kee.

Conversi, S. (2007) 'Homogenisation, nationalism and war: Should we still read Ernest Gellner?', *Nations and Nationalism*, 13(3): 371–94.

Cortés, G. (2019) 'Escaping the labyrinth of Roma political representation. Reflections on common citizenship', in G. Cortés and M. End (eds) *European Advocacy to Dimensions of Antigypsyism in Europe*, Brussels: European Network Against Racism, www.enar-eu.org/Book-Dimensions-of-Antigypsyism-in-Europe

Dunai, M. (2020) 'Living on margins, Hungary's Roma feel especially exposed to coronavirus', Reuters, www.reuters.com/article/us-health-coronavirus-hungary-roma/living-on-margins-hungarys-roma-feel-especially-exposed-to-coronavirus-idUSKBN21P238

EPHA (European Public Health Alliance) (2018) 'Closing the life expectancy gap of Roma in Europe', https://epha.org/wp-content/uploads/2018/10/closing-the-life-expectancy-gap-of-roma-in-europe.pdf

ERRC (European Roma Rights Centre) (2016) *Submission on the EU NRIS*, Budapest: ERRC, www.errc.org/uploads/upload_en/file/2015-eu-roma-framework-writen-comments-19-february-2016.pdf?utm_medium=email&utm_campaign=ERRC+submission+to+the+European+Commission+...&utm_source=YMLP&utm_term=

Fekete, L. (2016) 'Hungary: Power, punishment and the "Christian-national idea"', *Race & Class*, 57(4): 39–53.

Foucault, M. (2008) *The Birth of Biopolitics: Lectures at the Collège de France 1978–1979*, ed. M. Sennelart, trans. G. Burchell, Basingstoke: Palgrave.

FRA (Fundamental Rights Agency) (2014a) *Poverty and Employment: The Situation of Roma in 11 EU Member States; Roma Survey – Data in Focus*, Luxembourg: Publications Office of the European Union Fundamental Rights Agency.

FRA (2014b) *Education: The Situation of Roma in 11 EU Member States. Roma Survey – Data in Focus*, Luxembourg: Publications Office of the European Union Fundamental Rights Agency.

FRA (2014c) *Discrimination Against and Living Conditions of Roma Women in 11 EU Member States; Roma Survey – Data in Focus*, Luxembourg: Publications Office of the European Union.

FRA (2018) *Transition from Education to Employment of Young Roma in Nine EU Member States*, Luxembourg: Publications Office of the European Union.

Fraser, N. (1995) 'From redistribution to recognition? Dilemmas of justice in a "post-socialist" age', https://newleftreview.org/issues/I212/articles/nancy-fraser-from-redistribution-to-recognition-dilemmas-of-justice-in-a-post-socialist-age

Fraser, N. (2007) 'Identity, exclusion, and critique: A response to four critics', *European Journal of Political Theory*, 6(3): 305–38.

Friedlander, H. (1995) *Origins of Nazi Genocide: From Euthanasia to the Final Solution*, Chapel Hill, NC: University of North Carolina Press.

Gandhi, M.K. (1913) 'The collected works of Mahatma Gandhi' (vol 13), www.gandhiashramsevagram.org/gandhi-literature/collected-works-of-mahatma-gandhi-volume-1-to-98.php

Gheorghe, N. (2013) 'Choices to be made and prices to be paid: Potential roles and consequences in Roma activism and policy making', in W. Guy (ed) *From Victimhood to Citizenship: The Path of Roma Integration*, Budapest: Kossuth Kiado.

Giddens, A. (2014) *Turbulent and Mighty Continent: What Future for Europe?*, Cambridge: Polity.

Jones, B. and O'Donnell, M. (eds) (2018) *Alternatives to Neoliberalism: Towards Equality and Democracy*, Bristol: Policy Press.

Kamm, H. (1993) 'Havel calls the Gypsies "litmus test"', *The New York Times*, 10 December.

Klimova-Alexander, I. (2005) *The Romani Voice in World Politics: The United Nations and Non-State Actors*, Aldershot: Ashgate.

Landry, D. and MacLean, G. (1996) *The Spivak Reader*, New York, NY, and London: Routledge.

Law, I. and Kovats, M. (2018) *Rethinking Roma Identities, Politicisation and New Agendas*, London: Palgrave Macmillan.

Levitas, R (2005) *The Inclusive Society? Social Exclusion and New Labour*, Basingstoke: Palgrave.

Lister, R. (2004) *Poverty*, Cambridge: Polity Press.

Matache, M. and Bhabha, J. (2020) 'Anti-Roma racism is spiraling during COVID-19 pandemic', *Health and Human Rights Journal*, 7 April, www.hhrjournal.org/2020/04/anti-roma-racism-is-spiraling-during-covid-19-pandemic

Mudde, C. and Kaltwasser, C. (2017) *Populism: A Very Short Introduction*, Oxford: Oxford University Press.

Piketty, T. (2014) *Capital in the Twenty First Century*, Cambridge, MA: The Belknap Press of Harvard University Press.

Ryder, A. (2020) *Britain and Europe at a Crossroads: The Politics of Anxiety and Transformation*, Bristol: Bristol University Press.

Ryder, A. and Szilvasi, M. (2017) 'Marginality, activism and populism: The Roma and postcolonial Indian thinkers', *The Indian Journal of Social Work*, 78(1): 101–20.

Ryder, A. and Taba, M. (2018) 'Roma and social Europe', *The Journal of Poverty and Social Justice*, 17: 59–75.

Ryder, A., Cemlyn, S. and Acton, T. (2014) *Hearing the Voice of Gypsies, Roma and Travellers: Inclusive Community Development*, Bristol: Policy Press.

Saxer, M. (2020) 'It's the political economy, stupid!', *Social Europe*, 21 July, www.socialeurope.eu/its-the-political-economy-stupid?fbclid=IwAR1ncyPJJ_8LO0lw3-PqfOIIx-oYBAKdQQFYQi2DF8KiKEA3d9j67AUFBoE

Seikel, D. (2016) 'A social and democratic Europe? Obstacles and perspectives for action', WSI Working Papers 207, The Institute of Economic and Social Research (WSI), Hans-Böckler-Foundation.

Spivak, G.C. (2017) 'Can the subaltern speak?', in C. Nelson and L. Grossberg (eds) *Marxism and the Interpretation of Culture*, Urbana, IL: University of Illinois Press, pp 271–313.

Surdu, M. and Kovats, M. (2015) 'Roma identity as an expert-political construction', *Social Inclusion*, 3(5): 5–18.

Szeman, I. (2018) *Staging Citizenship: Roma, Performance and Belonging in EU Romania*, Oxford: Berghahn Books.

Trehan, N. (2001) 'In the name of the Roma? The role of private foundations and NGOs', in W. Guy (ed) *Between Past and Present: The Roma of Central and Eastern Europe*, Hatfield: University of Hertfordshire Press.

Trehan, N. (2009) 'Human rights entrepreneurship in post-Socialist Hungary: From "Gypsy problem" to "Romani rights"', PhD thesis, London School of Economics.

Trehan, N. and A. Kóczé (2009) 'Racism, (neo-)colonialism, and social justice: The struggle for the soul of the Romani movement in post-socialist Europe', in G. Huggan and I. Law (eds) *Racism Postcolonialism Europe*, Liverpool: Liverpool University Press, pp 50–74.

Turner, J. (2000) *The Tories and Europe*, Manchester and New York, NY: Manchester University Press.

van Baar, H. (2011) *The European Roma: Minority Representation, Memory and the Limits of Transnational Governmentality*, Amsterdam: F&N.

Van Barr, H. and Vermeersch, P. (2017) 'The limits of operational representations: Ways of seeing Roma beyond the recognition–redistribution paradigm', *Intersections: East European Journal of Society and Politics*, 3(4): 120–39.

van Baar, H., Ivasiuc, A. and Kreide, R. (eds) (2019) *The Securitization of the Roma in Europe*, London: Palgrave Macmillan.

Varoufakis, Y. (2015) 'How I became an erratic Marxist', *Guardian*, 18 February, www.theguardian.com/news/2015/feb/18/yanis-varoufakis-how-i-became-an-erratic-marxist

Varoufakis, Y. (2020) 'The EU coronavirus fund will take Europe another step towards disintegration', *Guardian*, 24 July.

Wilkinson, R. and Pickett, K. (2009) *The Spirit Level: Why Equality is Better for Everyone*, London: Penguin.

Williams, A., Gass, R., Horwitz, C., Vega-Frey, J., Maina, N. and Haines, S. (2010) *Framing Deep Change: Essays on Transformative Social Change*, Berkeley, CA: Third Way Press.

TWO

Mechanisms of empowerment for the Roma in a New Social Europe

Roland Ferkovics, Andrew Ryder and Marek Szilvasi

The context

Recent years have been turbulent for the European Union (EU), as evidenced by the UK's departure (Brexit) and increasing levels of Euroscepticism that charge the body with excessive bureaucracy and centralization. However, critics from the progressive spectrum of politics feel that the EU has neglected the social dimension and has lacked the energy and impetus of the Delors-led European Commission (EC) of 1985–95 in the realm of social policy. Indeed, it was under Delors that the EC established a Social Charter of the European Community and sought to steer the EU away from just being a free-trade area towards an expansive social contract-based market economy. Although there was a security and economic focus in the early manifestations of the EU (the Schuman Plan and the Common Market), alongside this has been a social dimension, in particular, after the Treaty of Amsterdam in 1997 strengthened EU competences in employment and social policy. Reflecting the dominance of the centre-right in

European politics, in particular, the European Peoples' Party, the EU institutions can be characterized as cautious in the social sphere, and the concept of Social Europe appears to have gone neglected for much of the past two decades (Graziano and Hartlaap, 2019). In part, this results from the EU's response to the financial and Eurozone crisis, and strategies within the EU centred on austerity, a point that is elaborated upon later in the chapter; however, there is also a long-standing tradition in many northern EU member states of exalting balanced budgets that deter stimulus and deficit spending.

In this context, we must assess what the EU has achieved for the Roma but also consider what new directions the EC might take under Ursula von der Leyen. This chapter seeks to dovetail a new Romani policy within a dynamic New Social Europe framework. In this respect, some 'blue sky thinking' – an envisioning of the future – will come into play. In an age of political and economic crisis, change and new directions often occur quickly and suddenly, presenting new opportunities. To date, it appears the Right have been the political beneficiaries of the crisis, and here we consider what Europe and the situation of the Roma might look like if progressive ideals prevail and a New Social Europe emerges.

Although the situation of the Roma has been on the agenda of EU institutions since the 1970s, the main concern of EU policymakers rested with the presumed itinerant way of life of some Romani and Traveller communities in Western Europe, and the Roma only received more substantive attention with the EU enlargement negotiations with Eastern Europe (Simhandl, 2006). The improvement of Romani rights became part of the criteria for accession. Romani civil society has also been instrumental in promoting this issue on the European stage through transnational activism; in part, it has found the EU more amenable to its advocacy than its more intransigent national governments, which, it has been hoped, the EU might guide, steer and, at times, prod into greater action. The most important European policy initiative for the Roma has been the EU Framework for National Roma Integration Strategies (NRIS) (hereafter referred to as the EU Roma Framework). The EU Roma Framework was adopted in 2011, requesting member states to develop NRIS or put in place an integrated set of policies (for countries with small Romani populations) to address Romani integration in core areas such as employment, education, health and housing. It relies on a soft form of governance known as the Open Method of Coordination (OMC), where it is believed that peer pressure and persuasion can help to steer member states to reach common goals. The adoption of the EU Roma Framework can be viewed as an adjunct to the EU 2020 Strategy, the response to the European economic crisis that also relies on OMC and involves an agenda for job creation and growth. The new EC is reviewing the Roma Framework and considering what steps should be taken in the future, and will unveil a new policy stance at the end of 2020. This chapter seeks to consider potential new actions.

The EU Roma Framework and mechanisms of empowerment

In re-conceptualizing Romani policy in Europe, we reflect on the successes and failures of the EU Roma Framework using Hennink et al's (2012) 'mechanisms of empowerment', a benchmark to measure inclusion and improve capacities.

The 'mechanisms' referred to include: **Knowledge**, in other words access to education, training and information from formal or other means such as experience and conscientisation. **Agency**, the capacity to act independently and make choices is another central mechanism enabling '*Self-Identity*', the self-confidence to achieve goals; '*Decision-Making*', the ability to make informed decisions; and '*Effecting Change*', the belief in one's own ability to take action. Another mechanism is **Opportunity Structure**, an enabling environment of social, economic, political, institutional and community support to foster community development. Capacity Building is another important dimension in this process referring to community capacity to provide or advocate for services or self-governance. According to Hennink et al, **Resources**, access to physical and financial resources, are integral to develop communities and empower. Finally, **Sustainability**, the ability of communities to develop initiatives towards long-term sustainability, is an integral part of empowerment.

It is important to differentiate between 'liberal empowerment' and 'liberating empowerment'. Liberal empowerment is often a feature of mainstream development agencies and organizations, and focuses on individual growth, though in an atomistic perspective, through the notion of the rational action of social actors based on individual interests. In contrast, liberating empowerment is a process where those denied the ability to make strategic life choices acquire such an ability in terms of resources, agency and achievements/outcomes through a process of conscientization/critical awareness and relying on collective action and structural change. Critics argue that the term 'empowerment' can be paternalistic as it implies an external body will grant empowerment; however, it is a term widely used by social justice campaigners, many of whom adopt a more radical interpretation. Hennink et al's (2012) 'mechanism of empowerment' clearly belongs to the more radical visioning of empowerment, and it is that conception that guides discussion in this chapter.

Hennink et al (2012) identify 'agency', as articulated through self-identity, decision-making and effecting change, as a central component in mechanisms of empowerment. This is one of the most serious criticisms of the EU Roma Framework, and actors within Romani civil society have consistently pointed out the lack of agency in developing national strategies and involvement in evaluating and monitoring progress (Ryder and Taba, 2018). Tokenism and paternalism within the EU Roma Framework have limited what Hennink et al (2012) describe as the ability to effect change, a sense of self-belief and, in turn, optimism. Romani civil society, especially that operating at the community and grass-roots level, has found the bureaucratic regulations of the EU difficult to navigate and has had limited success in accessing resources for capacity building; in contrast, those fortunate enough to attain funding have found themselves overwhelmed by the bureaucratic demands of the EU and/or to be merely 'token partners' in large consortia dominated by state institutions (ERGO, 2019). This is part of the continuation of 'internal colonialism' that Roma have experienced for centuries.

Disempowerment, as Hennink et al (2012) note, limits the opportunities to challenge power structures and venture into forms of meaningful co-production, as well as to enjoy forms of sustainability and autonomy that avoid reliance on short-term project funding that ties civil society to the rigid agenda of funders (Ryder et al, 2014). This is related to the idea of Gramscian 'hegemony', where the subject population actually accepts and normalizes its own disempowerment. A long-standing criticism of the EU is its propensity for top-down and distant policymaking that fails to effectively engage with or involve affected EU citizens. The EU has sought to embrace the concept of empowerment by adopting the '10 Basic Principles of Roma Inclusion', a tool for both policymakers and practitioners. The principles are centred on: (1) constructive, pragmatic and non-discriminatory policies; (2) explicit but not exclusive targeting; (3) an intercultural approach; (4) aiming for the mainstream; (5) awareness of the gender dimension; (6) transfer of evidence-based policies; (7) use of EU instruments; (8) involvement of regional and local authorities; (9) involvement of civil society; and (10) active participation of the Roma.

Despite an emphasis on participation, there is clearly a rhetoric–reality gap. For some commentators, the logic and rationale of Romani policymaking has been a narrow form of integration that fails to give the Roma a voice and seeks to problematize the Roma and promote assimilation (Szilvasi, 2015).

More fundamentally, there has been an absence of what Hennink et al (2012) describe as an 'opportunity structure': an enabling government willing to give financial support to inclusive community development steered by Romani communities. One indicator of a lack of progress is that in some EU countries, there are actually more unemployed Roma *after* nearly a decade of the EU Roma Framework being in operation – in 2019, 75 per cent of Roma were said to be unemployed, as opposed to 74 per cent in 2011 (Matarazzo and Naydenova, 2019). By contrast, in the same period, employment for the mainstream population has increased steadily in all countries surveyed. Likewise, there has been a deterioration in educational inclusion and housing, as well as expanding health inequalities for Roma. We can say that the Roma are the victims of 'structural racism': the normalization and legitimization of an array of dynamics – historical, cultural, institutional and interpersonal – that produces cumulative and chronic adverse outcomes. The evaluations by the EU Fundamental Rights Agency featured in Chapter One, with their disturbing social indicators, support this assertion. Why has progress been so limited overall?

For a start, in addition to grappling with the aftermath of a major financial crisis in 2008/09, Europe also had to contend with a Eurozone crisis that prompted a series of bailouts, as well as strict financial regulations and penalties to encourage balanced budgets. Austerity, as imposed by the 'troika' of the EC, the International Monetary Fund (IMF) and the European Central Bank, together with economic caution, has placed pressure on welfare budgets in many EU member states that has had adverse impacts on low-income groups like the Roma. Moreover, these policies defied conventional economic wisdom by slashing welfare and socio-economic development budgets at a time when economies were weak and vulnerable, consequently exacerbating unemployment and recession. Governments chose to bail out the banking system without demanding deep structural change, transferring the cost of this financial rescue onto ordinary citizens through spending cuts and increased regressive tax.

These economic ills have brought the EU to the precipice, creating a legitimacy crisis where a growing number of European citizens feel alienated from the EU, and it has been a major factor in the rise of the radical right (see Chapter Three by Taba). In the absence of governmental action to stimulate economies, some choose to accept the narratives of the radical right and nationalists that blame the status quo on actors such as the EU or migrants, and also demonize minority groups like the Roma, claiming that they are a financial and social burden on the state as a result of their alleged cultural dysfunctionality, often termed 'a culture of poverty' (Feischmidt et al, 2013) – a notion that taps into long-standing European racist tropes against the Roma termed as 'antigypsyism'. Structural racism, the rise of the radical right and forms of nativism and xenophobia in the public sphere have made the dominant conservative centre of Europe, such as the national parties within the European Peoples' Party (EPP), even more hesitant to actively promote the interests of groups like the Roma; hence, national action on 'integration' by member states has often failed to match the urgency and commitment of declarations issued by the EU.

Romani civil society has certainly raised its criticisms of the EU Roma Framework. Given that there is no binding nature to the EU Roma Framework, the design and implementation of the NRIS is absolutely dependent on political will, political priorities and the views of respective member states. Thus, there has been a serious lack of funding allocation, monitoring and proper implementation from the side of member states (REF, 2020). Critics of the EU Roma Framework also note some NRIS have a homogenized and even stereotypical view of the Roma and neglect the particular needs of Romani women, migrants and children (Rostas, 2019). Concerns on the lack of progress have prompted the EU to review the EU Roma Framework and the procedures for allocating EU funds for Romani inclusion and their outcomes (EC, 2020). The success of any new policy framework will depend on the degree to which policymakers and civil society accept and act upon the points of criticism raised thus far.

Questioning the rationale of Romani inclusion policy

EU Romani inclusion policies from 2011 to 2020 focused on how to bring Roma to the labour market and adequately validate their human resources through the exchange value system of the market. Within the introductory paragraph of the EU Roma Framework, Roma are repositioned from liberal citizens whose fundamental rights are systematically violated, to poorly educated future labour market entrants. The design of EU policies as recommended by the EU Roma Framework is based on inclusive labour market and activation schemes, which often run in parallel to the official labour market. Creating manual jobs with low-skill requirements and allocating them to unqualified and often uneducated Roma appears to be a key element in advancing Romani inclusion, according to the EU Roma Framework. Policymakers seem to believe that this will spontaneously further expand their inclusion in social, political and cultural spheres. Once the majority looks at Roma as citizens like themselves, as employees and taxpayers, this will have a correcting effect on accepting their cultural specificity and ensuring their civil and political equality.

However, a central question is whether all areas of the social life of Roma should be validated through the exchange value systems of the market and what the effects of the introduction of the logic of economic efficiency, profitability and competitiveness in the realm of civil liberties and political participation may be to the Romani situation. One of the identified contradictions lies in the definition of the labour market as the main field of inclusion. If the intent is to produce inclusion policies that would enable Roma to become fully fledged citizens, by considering the labour market as the main option, policymakers paradoxically chose one of the most rigid and disciplinary systems. The institution of the labour market is perceived as a fundamental organizational principle of our contemporary societies to such an extent that the lives of those people who are unable to become employed are considered futile. In the shift towards productivist policies at the EU level, which began with the Lisbon Agenda in 2000 and has been reinforced by the Europe 2020 Strategy, inclusion in the labour market is seen as the basic foundation upon which other inclusion policies can be built. Cultural, civil and political empowerment has been increasingly subordinated to market logic. This has implications for Roma and policies targeting them.

Roma road map

In February 2020, the EC published a 'road map' to facilitate consultation on a new Romani 'initiative'. In this document, the EC appeared to recognize some of the criticism levelled at the previous EU Roma Framework by pledging to combat both socio-economic exclusion and antigypsyism, and to promote Romani empowerment. In the initiative, the EC pledges to ask member states to better reflect diversity within the Romani population in their strategies, in particular, the needs of Romani women, children, youth, mobile EU citizens and migrants (DG Justice, 2020).

Will the finalized Romani initiative reflect calls for bolder initiatives backed up with hard law and aligned to a radical social policy agenda? The next section first outlines current civil society thinking and then outlines a series of concepts and ideas that have received relatively little discussion within Romani civil society.

Towards a Romani strategy

Leading voices in Romani civil society (Matarazzo and Naydenova, 2019) are calling for the development of a strategy based on hard law rather than OMC, with more ambitious and clearly defined targets, objectives and indicators, and with penalties for non-compliance (in June 2020, Romeo Franz MEP presented a draft resolution to the European Parliament Committee on Civil Liberties, Justice and Home Affairs (LIBE) calling for a Romani strategy with binding responsibilities for member states [Franz, 2020]). Calls have been made for a greater focus on antigypsyism and reference to gender, youth, Romani migrants and the promotion of minority targeting.

With reference to binding legislation, it should be noted that the Racial Equality Directive (RED) identifies Roma as a vulnerable ethnic group and the EU Roma Framework imposes an obligation on member states to desegregate public services like education. In this sense, more recognition is needed as to how the human rights of Roma in Europe are being undermined. The EC launched several infringement cases under the RED on the discrimination of Romani children in education in the Czech Republic (in 2014), Slovakia (in 2015) and Hungary (in 2016). Infringement can lead to the EU Court of Justice ruling that a member state must take action to comply with the Court of Justice judgment; it is a lengthy process as it takes time to gather data and scope is afforded to negotiate solutions. However, it is a cause of concern that the aforementioned cases have not been fully concluded. The midterm review of the EU Roma Framework by the EC (2018) notes there is a consensus that infringement proceedings as a tool should be further used to advance Romani integration. However, as noted, infringement proceedings have proven to be slow and cumbersome, with negative verdicts sometimes being ignored by member states. There is scope for such action outside of just segregated schooling and many would like to see legal action taken in, for example, the fields of housing, eviction and employment in Western as well as Eastern EU member states. The infringement process needs to be more transparent and faster, have improved monitoring, ensure compliance with basic human rights, and apply greater punitive sanctions.

Minority targeting

The initial development of the EU Roma Framework prompted an intense debate between national and European decision-makers and Romani civil society. Decision-makers asserted that any policy targeting Roma should be in line with the EC's approach, meaning that no future funding allocations should be based on 'ethnicity'. From the other side, civil society representatives countered with the argument that if there will be a Romani policy and, as a result, a funding allocation to reduce social and economic gaps without considering the target population as the main beneficiaries, then the risks of failing to reach out to the most excluded are high. Moreover, Romani civil society asserted that government should be 'explicit' in what they were going to do and how. The compromise between the two sides was to consider within the Common Basic Principles (a joint declaration between decision-makers and civil society, as discussed earlier) that one of the agreed principles be 'explicit but not exclusive'. The present experience has shown to many that governments have used this ambiguity to channel financial resources to places and localities where the Roma are demographically less evident. A re-evaluation of this approach is needed.

As part of the drive to achieve greater Romani inclusion, some lead civil society voices are calling for greater targeted projects and funding streams. However, some policymakers believe that developing specific inclusion policies for Romani populations runs counter to a 'mainstreaming approach'. To a certain degree, the viability of and/or support for targeting depends on the structure and political apparatus of the state, the composition of society, political history, the prevailing political attitude of governments, and so on. Care is needed with a targeted approach, in particular, to avoid the creation of inferior or ghettoized services. Furthermore, since Roma are often scapegoated, once targeted policies are designed, specific attention is needed to avoid further intentional exclusion of Roma. It has been argued that Romani inequality exists, in part, because of actual Romani-specific policies that fail to address and often reinforce a view of the Roma as an 'exceptional category'. Van Baar and Vermeersch (2017) suggest that measures that are aimed at 'saving' the Roma are implemented as part of a range of practices that mark Roma as vulnerable, leading to further essentialization and paternalism by the state.

A close relationship should exist between mainstream and targeted support so that knowledge arising from, for example, a local pilot project is then fed back into the daily operations of mainstream service providers and becomes part of their activities (Ryder et al, 2014). This can lead to progressive change within mainstream methods and approaches as the pilot facilitates new directions or becomes part of established services as a path to empowerment. In the next section, we discuss how inclusive forms of 'community development' can form part of a broad strategy to avert the dangers that can materialize when targeted actions become paternalistic and assimilatory.

The Youth Guarantee Scheme (YGS) is a commitment by EU member states to ensure that all young people under the age of 25 years receive a good-quality offer of employment, continued education, an apprenticeship or a traineeship within a period of four months of becoming unemployed or leaving formal education. Accordingly, member states are required to submit action plans as to how these goals can be achieved. Roma and other marginalized groups have been unable to access the benefits of this scheme to the same degree as more privileged peers; hence, greater targeting of Romani youth and improved outreach services should be a priority of active targeting. In 2021, the EC will present a Child Guarantee to make sure children have access to the services they need until adulthood (EC, 2020); again, targeted action for Romani children could be highly beneficial. Greater targeting and flexibility could also lead to improved outreach between service providers and Romani communities.

Blue sky thinking: on a New Social Europe

The EC is now reflecting a rationale for Romani inclusion initiatives based on economic as well as anti-discrimination and social justice principles. According to the EC road map, such efforts will help Roma achieve 'their potential to contribute to the economy, social protection systems and society at large ... the marginalization of Roma represents a loss of human capital, results in welfare dependence and limits labour supply and tax revenues' (DG Justice, 2020: 1–2). This is a robust argument against those who oppose Roma-targeted measures but we should not forget the logic of social justice in the application of a New Social Europe to Romani inclusion (on the concept, see Chapter One). Critics may be right that, for too long, the EU in general and its Romani inclusion policies in particular have been too growth-oriented and the social dimension has been subservient to competition and profitability.

A New Social Europe would recalibrate the relationship between economic interests and communities, placing greater emphasis on solidarity and social protection in a new social contract, linking the Roma more with social/economic rights discourses and processes, and mainstreaming them in EU institutions. It would also provide greater scope for Roma to shape policy.

Socio-economic rights

Most welfare systems have been closely tied with labour market participation (Bauman, 2005). The difference can be analytically cast between those policies that promote the right to labour as an aspect of welfare state services and those that promote the duty to labour as a foundation for all other socio-economic (and other) entitlements. The latter approach relies on processes of decommodification (Esping-Andersen, 1990), which enable decent living independent of the labour market. The former approach, on the contrary, relies on processes of re-commodification (Pierson, 2001), which aim to gradually tighten eligibility, roll back existing welfare provisions and promote the virtue of active re-engagement with the labour market.

The general manner of framing the debate on the just distribution of wealth is critical for the design of Romani inclusion policies. In left-wing circles, the universality of socio-economic rights and their primacy over other forms of rights is de rigueur. Socio-economic inclusion approaches do not accept the distribution of wealth as an entirely competitive or lottery-like matter, in which only the winning card gives an entitlement to provisions, while the gambling groups, which organized the game, get ever richer. They call for the entitlements for all citizens in some sort of egalitarian socio-economic (re)distribution. Building on liberal societies, in which civil and political rights are, at least formally, granted to all citizens regardless of their individual performance or merit, the left-wing discourse claims the same universal and unconditional application of socio-economic and cultural rights. According to Bauman (2005: 46), the welfare state 'rendered the right to dignified life a matter of political citizenship, rather than economic performance'.

The discourse on socio-economic inclusion understands the situation of injustice in terms of a socio-economic misdistribution. Different groups, sometimes delineated by racialized rhetoric, such as in the case of Roma, experience conditions of the relegated and unemployable underclass or exploited working class – the 'precariat', that is, those suffering from precarity (Standing, 2011). Therefore, policy solutions strictly favouring labour market integration might not have a tangible effect on the inclusion of these groups. It can be argued that welfare state inclusion policies are better placed to deal with the fully fledged inclusion of Roma, who are represented in large numbers among groups considered worthless to labour markets. However, socio-economic inclusion policies have been gradually shrinking alongside the contestation of the welfare state in the age of ever-growing austerity and declared scarcity. Pierson (2001) emphasizes that since the 1970s, welfare states have faced a context of essentially permanent austerity due to changes in global economies, the sharp slowdown in economic growth, the maturation of governments' commitments and population ageing, all factors that have generated enormous fiscal stress. This fiscal stress is based on the upward movement of surplus capital to the 1 per cent. In order to respond to this demographic and fiscal pressure, European welfare states began to initiate processes of recalibration, narrowing and tightening eligibility. Hence, from the beginning of the 1980s, according to Therborn (2008: 113), 'suddenly, the high water withdrew and was followed by a neoliberal tsunami ... and the privatization became the global order'. However, in the mid-1990s, a resurrected leftist discourse emerged in the shape of the alter-globalization movement and World Social Forums opposed to neoliberalism. This new global wave of leftist politics has sought to return social justice and socio-economic inclusion discourses to the main stage of policymaking.

A conceptual analysis of poverty and socio-economic inequalities within a human rights framework may have value for Romani policy frameworks given that political, civil, economic, social and cultural rights are connected and equally important for their mutual realization. Linking poverty, inequality and human rights creates an opening where the former concept can be understood and addressed in terms of the deprivation of capabilities or lack of empowerment, and as a denial and even a violation of human rights, a conception influenced by the 'capability approach' of Amartya Sen. Hence, a human rights framework can involve poverty strategies, a concrete parameter for providing legal remedies and measuring state compliance with international human rights obligations

(Prada, 2011). Such an approach might more effectively tackle the multiple and complex forms of exclusion experienced by the Roma but also perceive action to address such exclusion as a moral duty on the part of society rather than pathologizing and blaming the excluded.

A European New Deal would be a major component of a New Social Europe that targets the problems of involuntary migration, unemployment and low investment, all consequences of austerity, and tackles the regional economic disparities within the EU (Varoufakis and Galbraith, 2016). The New Deal would encompass a living wage centred, in part, on a jobs guarantee, as well as anti-poverty, social housing and environmental justice programmes ensuring a right to basic human needs and access to high-quality public services in health and education. These initiatives would be funded and supported by common European funds and would entail much more 'active' government economic initiatives encompassing forms of state intervention that some argue have been discouraged by the stipulations of the single market within the EU.

Active employment measures should avoid statist solutions of large public works programmes, as practised in Hungary, which confined Roma to low-skilled and low-paid work (ERRC, 2015). Involving Roma in large infrastructure projects can be effective if coupled with genuine skills development and space for upward mobility. On account of the high levels of discrimination in the waged labour market, many Roma prefer or are compelled to engage in small-scale entrepreneurial activities. Despite the EU Roma Framework promoting microcredit, the success of such initiatives has been limited; some have been discouraged by the terms and conditions of loans, or have lacked the financial and technical expertise to start up a business. There is also the danger that when implemented under a neoliberal framework, microcredit can actually increase indebtedness and marginalization (Bateman, 2014). There are isolated cases of civil society providing financial and business start-up mentoring and guidance, a notable case being the Autonomia Foundation in Hungary; such work needs to be scaled up. There is also a need to promote greater awareness and understanding of development finance, where local communities support, encourage and catalyse community development and expansion through public and private investment, which should be premised on egalitarianism, self-empowerment and growth, rather than on neoliberal principles centred on repayment generating profit.

A New Social Europe would entail greater reinforcement and implementation of the principles of the European Pillar of Social Rights that seeks to bring 'fairness' into the lives of European citizens (EC, 2020). The European Pillar of Social Rights is likely to have an important impact on EU Roma policy. Proclaimed by all EU institutions in 2017, the 20 principles of the European Pillar of Social Rights aim at improving equal opportunities and jobs for all, fair working conditions, social protection, access to services, and gender equality (EC, 2020). Part of a New Social Europe would also entail the European Social Union (ESU), a 'coming-together' process involving welfare states that would facilitate mutual adaptation based on jointly defined criteria and would include risk-pooling. Given the EU has its own budget and resources, the foundations are there for forms of social federalism; however, this may ultimately entail the need for new forms of EU tax consolidation powers. Hemerijck (2013) has defined the ESU as a holding environment: in other words a zone of resilience centred on shared values and a common purpose, backed up by competent institutions, ready to act in times of crisis and adaptation. Thus, a holding environment should mitigate stress and tensions and consequently uphold the integrity of national welfare states. The global economic system has become highly complex and difficult to regulate, in part, because of financialization; the power and dominance of financial investment, free market thinking centred on deregulation and privatization have empowered global finance and helped it prosper and take over aspects of the state, such as welfare and social care (Citizens for Financial Justice, 2019). Clearly, if there is to be a meaningful ESU and a holding environment, these trends need to be challenged at the European level.

An obvious and key question is: where will the money come from and how will it be channelled to need? The EC relaxed the budgetary constraints stemming from the Maastricht criteria, setting a precedent for further relaxation. Soros (2013) has argued that if EU member states could convert their entire stock of government debt into Eurobonds, then indebted and poor member states' budgets could move into surplus and fiscal stimulus would replace austerity. More recently, Soros (2020) has proposed that the EU should raise the money needed for a European Recovery Fund to deal with the economic consequences of COVID-19 by selling 'perpetual bonds' on which the principal does not have to be repaid (though they can be repurchased or redeemed at the issuer's discretion). As perpetual bonds never have to be repaid, they would impose a surprisingly light fiscal burden on the EU, despite the considerable financial firepower they would mobilize.

With reference to EU funding, there have been calls for respect for and compliance with the principles of equality and social protection to constitute an element of conditionality in EU funding streams (André, 2009). An element of conditionality has started to be introduced to EU funding but compliance with the European Pillar of Social Rights, with an impact on funding, could be a mechanism to drive up social convergence. Increased employment participation and the consequent increase in purchasing power will also raise the overall tax take and correspondingly reduce welfare payment demands. To start with, the EU should embrace progressive taxation and close the loopholes that enable tax avoidance. The measures this section has outlined are 'pre-distributive' forms of social investment that rest on the logic that it is more cost effective to ensure marginalization does not occur in the first place than to use resources to tackle and mitigate the impact of poverty and exclusion. The acceptance of such a notion would have profound consequences for Romani communities. The active economic and social interventions envisaged in this section certainly align with Hennink et al's (2012) vision of opportunity structure and enabling government.

Agency and community organizing

For some, notions of a New Social Europe, as outlined earlier, might conjure up fears of statism, a form of top-down governance that is distant and bureaucratic. For Roma, in the past, such regimes under communism constituted forms of assimilation and control. In contrast, a New Social Europe would need to be driven by empowered and active communities, including those like the Roma at the margins. In a New Social Europe, Romani policies need to be inherently flexible and, where appropriate, involve forms of minority targeting that can shape mainstream policy and be designed and implemented through negotiation and co-production with civil society and or staff employed in public and targeted initiatives. However, concerns have been expressed as to the degree of autonomy such initiatives afford and the tensions that can arise when Roma are employed by state institutions and services that arouse hostility and mistrust on the basis of past discrimination. Here, civil society could play an invaluable role in performing such tasks, ensuring Romani expertise helps shape and deliver inclusive public services in meaningful forms of co-production. However, as noted, Romani communities and civil society are perilously weak at the moment and need huge levels of financial support and competence to enable localized and organic community development but in a way that also allows local community groups scope to build capacity within Romani communities, acting in the sense of the writings of Paulo Freire (1972) as catalysts for critical awareness and community organization. Hennink et al (2012) refer to such awareness as conscientization. Conscientization can be linked to a 'Development Education and Awareness Raising' (DEAR) approach common with non-governmental organization (NGO) projects in the Global South, which provides communities with tools to critically engage in development issues, and mobilizes greater public support for action against poverty and exclusion.

Trehan (2001) raised concerns about the funding and donor-driven agendas in Europe that run the danger of creating forms of managerialism (NGO-ization) that disempower Romani activists. Alinsky (1971) cautioned as to the dangers of activism being hijacked by a service-driven agenda. Indeed, forms of co-production and public–private partnerships between Romani civil society/institutions and governmental agencies need to take care to avoid becoming an adjunct of the state in forwarding agendas that are assimilatory. Reflecting such fears, a policy briefing by the University of Manchester (2014) stated that interventions by third sector agencies entrusted with managing interaction between Roma and local institutions held the long-term risk of perpetuating the Roma's dependency on outside mediators and support provisions. Instead, it was argued, intervention should take the form of capacity building within the Romani community, enabling them to develop expertise and competences beyond the community outreach work. This critique mirrors the thoughts of theorists such as Foucault (1991), who argued that development theory constitutes a form of control, through the concept of governmentality, which normalizes neoliberal and assimilative policy agendas, and 'responsibilizes', individualizes and pathologizes the victims.

Some of the concerns outlined earlier are theorized by Powell (2010), who contrasts two interpretations of intervention/development. One perspective perceives social policy intervention as assimilationist, based on the imposition of civilizing values that discard Romani norms and values; in contrast, others see such intervention as a means to forward equity and competence through emancipatory processes. The emancipatory perspective argues that formal education, for example, broadens horizons and opportunities, allowing Romani children to escape and reformulate the stifling straightjacket of tradition, and have agency. Critics argue that this can constitute a narrow form of integration that ultimately assimilates. A danger, though, is that an unquestioning exaltation of ethnicity can promote static and narrow versions of identity that ignore the fluidity of identity and Romani propensity for 'bricolage' or cultural borrowing and innovation. The key point is that inclusion has to be shaped and negotiated, with active involvement of and leadership from the Roma themselves (Bogdan et al, 2015).

Social accountability

Some Romani NGOs are able to enter into forms of co-production and retain autonomy; by autonomy, we mean not only the ability to have a significant say in the design and delivery of policy, but also a chance to challenge and offer critique. However, such groups often enjoy extensive experience, thematic expertise and engaged communities, holding authorities accountable about the terms and direction of any service. Social accountability is an evolving umbrella category that includes citizen monitoring and oversight of public and/or private sector performance, user-centred public information access and dissemination systems, public complaint and grievance redress mechanisms, and citizen participation in actual resource allocation decision-making, such as participatory budgeting (Joshi and Houtzager, 2012). The approach refers to strategies developed over the last two decades that employ information and participation to demand fairer and more effective public services (Maru, 2010). It seeks to improve institutional performance by bolstering collective citizen engagement in and monitoring of public policy systems and the public responsiveness and effectiveness of the state (Fox,

2014). It should be noted that a critique of this approach is that participation is based more on the ideas of 'governance' and 'accountability' of citizens in terms of oversight; it does not link back to the citizen having a claim to certain social/economic rights. However, 'social accountability' is a term that governments and donors agree to use, and it can be used as a bridge to include wider civil society and rights-based demands into the framework.

To achieve such reorientation in a New Social Europe, a complete cultural and organizational paradigm shift would need to occur that would validate community as a source of determination and knowledge. Here, rather than the government using civil society as a tool to impose narrow inclusion/assimilation policies, we see a situation where civil society is in the driving seat instead, directing governmental and institutional power as to what needs to be done. This point reiterates a central argument in this chapter that an effective 'Social Europe' approach for Romani communities requires greater support for the development and expansion of Romani civil society in a manner that extends not only its capacity and skills, but also its autonomy. Hence, support and encouragement would be given to community organizing, social accountability and 'inclusive community development', where allocated resources allow for independent manoeuvrability and bottom-up development, in which a premium is placed on empowerment and agency, as well as asset-based development, where community traditions are adapted and used as a foundation for development (Ryder et al, 2014). Such inclusivity would certainly facilitate the agency and self-belief that Hennink et al (2012) believe is key to inclusion.

Another means of ensuring community and civil society voices are heard and acted on is to create a second chamber of the EU featuring representatives of cities, regions and NGOs, such as trade unions and community organizations (Zielonka, 2019). This body should have equal status to the European Parliament and include Romani civil society as the

Romani cause has been hampered by the low level of Romani representation in the European Parliament and the limitations of the Roma Platform – the annual meetings between Romani civil society and the EC.

Inclusive community development is, in part, dependent on knowledge production, research and data that allow an understanding of the issues communities face, assess the impact of existing policy frameworks and interventions, and help to formulate new policy tools. Social accountability and community monitoring should be an important part of the next EU Roma Framework and allocation of resources. Limited resources have impeded the scope of such work in measuring the impact and relevance of policy, and in some cases, member states refuse to collect ethnically disaggregated data. With EU funding, the Central European University Roma Civil Monitor was able to build civil society networks in EU member states to assess the impact of the NRIS and EU Roma Framework. It has conducted valuable monitoring and helps empower Romani activists by training them in monitoring processes. However, resources have been relatively slight and not permitted more collaborative and participatory forms of monitoring and research or pioneering leadership of Romani community members in research design, data collection and analysis. The EU needs to greatly extend the level of resources accorded to such work in the new policy cycle on Roma.

Intersectionality and solidarity

The Romani movement has been able to galvanize and mobilize sections of Romani civil society through forms of 'identity politics'; critics would argue it has, at times, essentialized and sought to homogenize Romani identity, as evidenced through 'nation-building' efforts (Surdu and Kovats, 2015). For example, in 2000, the fifth World Romani Congress in Prague appealed through its president, Emil Ščuka, for the

Roma to be recognized as a nation without territory; such nation-building constructs have enjoyed limited support or even awareness from Romani communities, and have tended to be driven by small Romani political elites (McGarry, 2010). However, ethnicity and identity have been effective tools in binding forms of Romani transnational activism and solidarity, which has been instrumental in the relative success of Romani advocacy at the European level. The question has been raised as to whether an overt focus on identity politics has diverted Romani activists from the need for fundamental structural change. Has Romani civil society aligned itself too closely to tokenist policy change that offers merely cosmetic change? This debate has relevance for Nancy Fraser's (1995) discussions on how in 'post-socialist' societal conflicts, group identity has tended to supplant class interest as the locus of political debate and contestation. The message of this chapter is that Fraser is right to contend that struggles for recognition have validity and can help achieve incremental change but the quest for redistribution is central for meaningful change to come about. To date, Romani civil society has conducted limited discussion on the centrality of redistribution and what a New Social Europe might mean, as well as on how issues related to ethnic identity would be addressed within such a policy framework.

However, evidence of a paradigm shift within Romani civil society is seen in growing support for intersectionality, where Roma show solidarity and form alliances with women's, lesbian, gay, bisexual, trans and queer (LGBTQ), migrants, and other marginalized groups. Romani empowerment could thus be interpreted as Roma and non-Roma finding common points of interest and forming alliances. Such intersectionality has challenged narrow notions of Romani identity that exalt conservative tradition and insular forms of bonding social capital. Such intersectionality is more apparent among the cadre of national/international Romani leaders and is less apparent at the local level; more, though, is needed to be done to align the Romani struggle with broader social justice and anti-poverty campaigns directed at multidimensional poverty (such as poor health, lack of education, inadequate living standards, disempowerment, poor quality of work and so on), as well as support an understanding of green/environmental issues, where Roma can identify common interests in the mainstream and give new focus to Romani issues.

Given climate change and the environmental challenges that society now faces, an important part of a New Social Europe and, indeed, Romani inclusion strategies will rest upon sustainability and a new 'Green Deal' ensuring economic activity seeks to not only stem, but also reverse, the harm already inflicted upon the planet. Romani activism should more robustly engage with environmental and climate justice movements, not only to challenge the context of environmental injustice and racism endured by Roma, but also to build solidarities and knowledge to tackle global challenges. Previous periods of major social investment and active economic interventions by the welfare state, such as that which occurred from 1945 to the early 1970s, witnessed rapid growth. Such a model may not be sustainable environmentally because of the level of resources that were and would be devoured to fuel such growth. In addition, post-war growth was also based on cheap materials and exploitation of low-wage labour from regions of the periphery. Within a New Social Europe and hopefully a corresponding new globalized economic order, such actions could not be replicated. Furthermore, technological advancements and the increasing automation of production and services might mean full employment is also an impossible goal in the sense that it materialized in the post-war period. Hence, a New Social Europe will necessitate sustainable forms of production that could, in fact, generate new green industries and lead to the redistribution of working hours as well as resources.

The proposed recalibration of the role of the EU and the values it should promote centred on social justice will also entail new conceptions of European citizenship built upon a notion of 'inclusive European citizenship'. Inclusive citizenship encompasses solidarity, or a belief in the capacity to act in unity with others in their claims for justice and recognition; thus, it complements well the policy agenda of a New Social Europe (Donaldson and Kymlicka, 2017). Inclusive citizenship should articulate the terms of when it is fair for people to be treated the same and when it is fair that they should be treated differently. In this sense, it should not have the rigidity of, say, French conceptions of citizenship that preclude minority ethnic targeting and affirmative action. In addition, recognition – framed in terms of the intrinsic worth of all human beings, as well as recognition of and respect for their differences – should be a core value in inclusive citizenship and power should act decisively where such principles are challenged. Self-determination should also be part of the formula of inclusive citizenship, allowing people the ability to exercise some degree of control over their lives; hence, this chapter has advocated radical forms of Romani empowerment.

Conclusion

Although EC President Ursula von der Leyen has affirmed a strong determination to present an action plan to deliver on the European Pillar of Social Rights, it remains to be seen whether radical measures are initiated as a part of a process of building a New Social Europe. The EC is aware that it faces a legitimacy crisis, as reflected by the rise of the radical right, and that additional mistakes could further the growth of political extremism and xenophobia. Furthermore, the EU and the current European social model is under threat from militant forms of neoliberalism fused with populism as the US with Trump and Britain through 'Brexit' seek to reorient their economic models in order to maintain an advantage over old and emerging competitors, and to retain hegemony in the core group of economic powers. To avoid a 'race to the bottom' – a downward spiral of social protections, wages and workers' rights – the EU will need to hold firm in defence of the European social model and initiate a bold and dynamic reorientation of the European project through a New Social Europe. The COVID-19 pandemic and the economic crisis it has induced necessitate major acts of economic intervention and stimulus. The mood and support for transformative change are therefore far greater than some European leaders in recent times have assumed. Through Hennink et al's (2012) 'mechanism of empowerment', we have sought to promote a vision of a New Social Europe that offers economic fairness with the potential for skills development, coupled with increased scope for agency, knowledge, opportunity and capacity building.

In October 2020, the EC unveiled the 'EU Roma Strategic Framework for Equality, Inclusion and Participation', which refers to infringement action to tackle antigypsyism, a drive to cut poverty and empower Roma. However, some critics felt it lacked binding legal obligations, and it remains to be seen if the bold vision of transformative change as set out in this chapter materializes.

References

Alinsky, S. (1971) *Rules for Radicals: A Political Primer for Practical Radicals*, New York, NY: Random House.

André, M.H. (2009) 'Social Europe and the Lisbon strategy', *Transfer: European Review of Labour and Research*, 15(1): 147–9.

Bateman, M. (2014) 'A New Balkan Tragedy? The Case of Microcredit in Bosnia', http://blogs.lse.ac.uk/lsee/2014/04/08/a-new-balkan-tragedy-the-case-of-microcredit-in-bosnia/

Bauman, Z. (2005) *Work, Consumerism, and the New Poor*, Maidenhead: Open University Press.

Bogdán, M., Jekatyerina, D., Tímea, J., Kóczé, A., Rövid, M., Rostas, I., Ryder, A., Szilvási, M. and Taba, M. (eds) (2015) 'Nothing about us without us? Roma participation in policy making and knowledge production', European Roma Rights Centre, www.errc.org/roma-rights-journal/roma-rights-2-2015-nothing-about-us-without-us-roma-participation-in-policy-making-and-knowledge-production

Citizens for Financial Justice (2019) 'Spotlight on financial justice: Understanding global inequalities to overcome financial injustice', funded by the European Union, https://citizensforfinancialjustice.org/resource/spotlight-on-financial-justice-understanding-global-inequalities-to-overcome-financial-injustice/

DG Justice (2020) 'Initiative setting out the EU post-2020 Roma equality and inclusion policy', https://ec.europa.eu/info/law/better-regulation/have-your-say/initiatives/12191-EU-post-2020-Roma-policy

Donaldson, S. and Kymlicka, W. (2017) 'Inclusive citizenship beyond the capacity contract', in A. Shachar, I. Bloemraad, M. Vink and R. Bauböck (eds) *Oxford Handbook of Citizenship*, Oxford: Oxford University Press.

EC (European Commission) (2018) Report on the evaluation of the EU Framework for National Roma Integration Strategies up to 2020, Brussels, EC, https://eur-lex.europa.eu/legal-content/EN/TXT/PDF/?uri=CELEX:52018DC0785&from=EN

EC (2020) 'Communication and annex on a strong Social Europe for just transitions', https://ec.europa.eu/commission/presscorner/detail/en/fs_20_49

ERGO (European Roma Grassroots Organisations) (2019) 'Community-Led Local Development (CLLD) for Roma inclusion – Synthesis report', http://ergonetwork.org/

ERRC (European Roma Rights Centre) (2015) 'Submission to UN UPR on Hungary', www.errc.org/cms/upload/file/hungary-submission-un-upr-september-2015.pdf

Esping-Andersen, G. (1990) *The Three Worlds of Welfare Capitalism*, Princeton, NJ: Princeton University Press.

Feischmidt, M., Szombati, K. and Szuhay, P. (2013) 'Collective criminalization of the Roma in Central and Eastern Europe' in S. Body-Gendrot, M. Hough, K. Kerezsi, R. Lévy and S. Snacken (eds) *The Routledge Handbook of European Criminology*, Abingdon: Routledge.

Foucault, M. (1991) 'Governmentality' (trans R. Braidotti and revised by C. Gordon), in G. Burchell, C. Gordon and P. Miller (eds) *The Foucault Effect: Studies in Governmentality*, Chicago, IL: University of Chicago Press, pp 87–104.

Fox, J. (2014) 'Social accountability: What does the evidence really say?', Global Partnership for Social Accountability (GPSA), https://gpsaknowledge.org/knowledge-repository/ social-accountability-what-does-the-evidence-really-say-2/ #.VVu9T0ZAowA

Franz, R. (2020) 'Presentation to the European Parliament Committee on Civil Liberties', 4 June, https:// multimedia.europarl.europa.eu/de/libe-committee- meeting_20200604-1645-COMMITTEE-LIBE_vd?fbcli d=IwAR2qaYY7wgwvM1fStLd3Yq8QdXONFG2D_8MnDC- PxKthBRwiQ_bV75TTIUU

Fraser, N. (1995) 'From redistribution to recognition? Dilemmas of justice in a "postsocialist" age', *New Left Review*, 212 (July/August): 68–93.

Freire, P. (1972) *Pedagogy of the Oppressed*, Harmondsworth and New York, NY: Penguin Books.

Galbraith, J. and Varoufakis, Y. (2016) 'Toward a European New Deal questionnaire for DiEM25 members', https://diem25.org/ wp-content/uploads/2016/09/160920_DiEM25_European_ New_Deal_Questionnaire_English_Final.pdf

Graziano, P. and Hartlapp, M. (2019) 'The end of social Europe? Understanding EU social policy change', *Journal of European Public Policy*, 26(10): 1484–501.

Hemerijck, A. (2013) *Changing Welfare States*, Oxford: Oxford University Press.

Hennink, M., Kiiti, N., Pillinger, M. and Jayakaran, R. (2012) 'Defining empowerment: Perspectives from international development organisations', *Development in Practice*, 22(2): 202–15.

Joshi, A. and Houtzager, P. (2012) 'Widgets or Watchdogs? Conceptual explorations in social accountability', *Public Management Review*, 14(2: special issue: 'The Politics and Governance of Public Services in Developing Countries'): 145–62.

McGarry, A. (2010) *Who* Speaks *for* Roma*? Political Representation of a Transnational Minority Community*, New York: Continuum.

Maru, V. (2010) 'Allies unknown: Social accountability and legal empowerment', *Health and Human Rights*, 12(1), www.hhrjournal.org/2013/08/allies-unknown-social-accountability-and-legal-empowerment/

Matarazzo, M. and Naydenova, V. (2019) *Post-2020 EU Roma Strategy: The Way Forward*, Berlin: Open Society Foundation, https://www.opensocietyfoundations.org/publications/post-2020-eu-roma-strategy-the-way-forward

Pierson, P. (ed) (2001) *The New Politics of the Welfare State*, Oxford: Oxford University Press.

Powell, R. (2010) 'Gypsy-Travellers and welfare professional discourse: On individualisation and social integration', *Antipode*, 43(2): 471–93.

Prada, F.M. (2011) *Empowering the Poor Through Human Rights Litigation*, Paris: UNESCO.

REF (Roma Education Fund) (2020) 'Roma Education Fund's response to Roma policy: Tackling discrimination and socio-economic exclusion' (submission to European Commission consultation), https://ec.europa.eu/info/law/better-regulation/have-your-say/initiatives/12191-EU-post-2020-Roma-policy/F509051

Rostas, I. (2019) *A Task for Sisyphus: Why Europe's Roma Policies Fail*, Budapest: Central European University Press.

Ryder, A. and Taba, M. (2018) 'Roma and Social Europe', *The Journal of Poverty and Social Justice*, 17(special edition: 'Roma in a Time of Paradigm Shift and Chaos'): 59–75.

Ryder, A., Cemlyn, S. and Acton, T. (eds) (2014) *Hearing the Voice of Gypsies, Roma and Travellers: Inclusive Community Development*, Bristol: Policy Press.

Simhandl, K. (2006) '"Western Gypsies and Travellers" – "Eastern Roma": The creation of political objects by the institutions of the European Union', *Nation and Nationalism*, 12(1): 97–115.

Soros, G. (2013) 'How to save the European Union', *The Guardian*, 9 April, www.theguardian.com/business/2013/apr/09/eurozone-crisis-germany-eurobonds

Soros, G. (2020) 'The EU should issue perpetual bonds', Project Syndicate, 20 April, www.project-syndicate.org/commentary/finance-european-union-recovery-with-perpetual-bonds-by-george-soros-2020-04

Standing, G. (2011) *Precariat: The New Dangerous Class*, New York, NY: Bloomsbury Academic.

Surdu, M. and Kovats, M. (2015) 'Roma identity as an expert-political construction', *Social Inclusion*, 3(5): 5–18.

Szilvasi, M. (2015) 'Roma and the contradictions of European inclusion policies: Citizens associated with European societies', PhD thesis, University of Aberdeen.

Therborn, G. (2008) *From Marxism to Post-Marxism?*, London: Verso.

Trehan, N. (2001) 'In the name of the Roma', in W. Guy (ed) *Between Past and Future: The Roma of Central and Eastern Europe*, Hatfield: University of Hertfordshire Press, pp 134–49.

University of Manchester (2014) 'Roma migrants from Central and Eastern Europe', https://hummedia.manchester.ac.uk/faculty/policy/Policy@Manchester-briefing---Roma-Migrants.pdf

Van Baar H. and Vermeersch, P. (2017) 'The limits of operational representations', *Intersections: East European Journal of Society and Politics*, 3(4): 120–39.

Varoufakis, Y. and Galbraith, J. (2016) 'Toward a European New Deal', DiEM25, https://diem25.org/wp-content/uploads/2016/09/160920_DiEM25_European_New_Deal_Questionnaire_English_Final.pdf

Zielonka, J. (2019) 'Europe's future: Democracy and equality should come first', Social Europe, 25 June, www.socialeurope.eu/democracy-and-equality

THREE

Antigypsyism in a time of neoliberalism: challenging the radical right through transformative change

Marius Taba

Introduction

The chapter explores the rise of radical-right populism and authoritarianism and the implications for Roma. It critiques and seeks to refashion the strategies and frames used by anti-racists and Romani rights champions ranged against antigypsyism in a way that will enhance the potential for intersectional solidarity, dialogue and alignment with the concept of a New Social Europe (for a discussion of this concept, see Chapter One). This chapter argues for legal protections and human rights to be defended and upheld. However, the narrative directed by rights 'champions' at combating antigypsyism should also be focused on Romani potential, emphasizing the capacities of Roma in a social, political and economic sense, and leading to forms of empowerment; this is a central theme of this book. It is also argued that the process of tackling antigypsyism, which is a specific form of racism towards the Roma centred on tropes such as criminality and cultural dysfunctionality, warrants transformative change (for a definition, see Chapter One) given the deep structural, cultural and institutional locus of racism, including antigypsyism, and the inflammation of such in the economic crises and convulsions so redolent of late capitalism.

Crisis and irrationality

The writer and philosopher George Santayana (2006: 32) famously said: 'Those who cannot remember the past are condemned to repeat it.' The wonderful thing about history is that it is sometimes a guide to the future rather than just a record of the past. In his path-breaking book *The Great Transformation*, Karl Polanyi (1944: 236) reflected on the rise of European fascism in the 1930s and noted: '[T]he moment would come when both the economic and the political systems were threatened by complete paralysis. Fear would grip the people, and leadership would be thrust upon those who offered an easy way out at whatever ultimate price. The time was ripe for the fascist solution.' According to Polanyi, a country approaching the fascist phase showed symptoms such as irrational philosophies, racialist aesthetics, anti-capitalist demagogy, criticism of the party system and widespread disparagement of the status quo. Despite its revolutionary rhetoric, this was a sham (false) rebellion, arranged with the tacit approval of the authorities, where new alliances were formed between the fascists, the establishment and economic elites (Polanyi, 1944: 238).

As discussed in Chapter One, populism is an offshoot of nationalism; some present-day observers fear that authoritarian populism in Europe may be the precursor to new forms of fascism and may normalize the politics of the extreme right (Ryder, 2020). Mudde (2018b), with reference to the growth of populism, notes:

> The great recession that followed the 2008 financial crash freed populism from the (radical) right. The rise of

Syriza in Greece, and to a lesser extent Podemos in Spain, showed clear similarities with, but also fundamental differences from, the populist radical right. They shared a pro-people and anti-elite politics, but Podemos and Syriza were clearly part of the radical left, both in terms of ideology and subculture.

The dominant European forms of populism that have emerged have been associated with the radical right. Fascism and contemporary radical-right populism share some similar traits. Both present a homogenizing view of 'the people' and conceive of political opponents as 'the anti-people' (Mudde and Kaltwasser, 2017). In general, populism follows an ideology that considers society to be separated into two homogeneous and antagonistic groups, often centred on the 'the pure people' versus 'the corrupt elite', and the need to follow the 'will' of the people. The homogenizing views of populism are grounded in nationalist thinking and symbolism. In considering such polarization, it is worth discussing the ideas of the controversial theorist Carl Schmitt, a key thinker active during and sympathetic towards National Socialism in Germany; despite his sympathies with the regime, his influence extended into the post-war period. Schmitt envisaged a 'pure difference' between the 'self' and 'other' developing through what can be described as an 'agonism' that had nation-building potential by marking the boundaries between insiders and outsiders (Roskamm, 2015). Agonism is the intense contestation by rival camps of their adversaries' values and identities; it fragments social cohesion, deepening and reifying the identities of the besieged adversaries (Dryzek and Niemeyer, 2006). Agonism is a phenomenon that deploys binary speech acts, irrationalism and manipulation. For Schmitt (1996), a national identity could only be constituted by the suppression of the adversary. Schmitt's concept of 'us and them' (friend and foe) – the marker between those classified as belonging to the national group and those outside the boundary – was nationalistic and sympathetic to fascist ideals. The Schmittian form of agonism creates a public enemy who ultimately cannot be engaged with in partnership, but only be vanquished (Edwards, 2013).

Mudde (2007) has described ethno-nationalist radical-right parties as largely overlapping with the populist radical right. They have at their core a strong 'charismatic' leader, a 'warrior' who can lead the people into binary, Manichaean contests against internal and external enemies. Mudde (2018a: 254) claims that ethnic or racial types of civil wars and pogroms are most evident in Eastern Europe but there are examples where Roma have become victims of radicalism in Western Europe too. There is increasing evidence of the Roma being cast by the radical populist and nationalist right as an internal enemy and external threat located outside of the boundary of the national group (see Chapter Four by Rorke).

As noted in Chapter One, the response to the COVID-19 pandemic has highlighted the nature and reach of antigypsyism in Europe, as well as how the state and a broad spectrum of political actors can orchestrate anti-Romani sentiments. In addition to general measures to prevent the spread of COVID-19, authorities in Slovakia, Romania and Bulgaria introduced additional restrictions to put Romani communities under strict quarantine, sometimes resorting to the use of police and military force. Amnesty International (2020) reports that in Bulgaria and Slovakia, the state authorities have argued that such measures are necessary for the protection of public health and safety. State intervention during the pandemic crisis has demonstrated how Romani identities have been securitized and problematized in such a way to make anti-Romani discourses seem 'reasonable' rather than offensive (Van Baar, 2011b). These actions were shaped by age-old racist perceptions of the Roma as carriers of disease.

Manifestations of antigypsyism by the radical right and state are not just to be found in Central and Eastern Europe. Prior to the pandemic, forced evictions in countries such as Italy and France raised considerable concern from the Romani rights movement. For instance, in France, a secret government circular was leaked in 2010 and revealed a targeted policy to prioritize the deportation of Romani migrants, among other groups (Parker, 2012). The Conservative government of Boris Johnson pledged in the general election of 2019 to enforce a crackdown on nomadism, an action that was seen by some to be a cynical attempt to instrumentalize antigypsyism (Monbiot, 2019). Antigypsyism is to be found within mainstream governments as well as on the part of the radical right; however, the rise of the radical right encourages forms of shadowing and mimicry by a mainstream eager to conserve power and pander to anti-Romani sentiments.

Authoritarian and radical-right populism is a political force that downplays the separation of powers, the independence and legitimacy of a free press, and the rule of law. With authoritarian populism, though, unlike with fascism, democracy is challenged and undermined but not destroyed, which can potentially normalize extreme-right politics and prepare the ground for its wider acceptance (Mudde, 2018a). In discussing radical-right populism, it is worth reappraising Adorno's (1948) comments on the study he participated in: 'The authoritarian personality' (Adorno et al, 1950). The study sought to identify key personality traits inclined towards authoritarianism that might make some susceptible to embracing fascism in a crisis. For Adorno (1948: 129), fascism is a form of irrationalism as its consequences are contrary to the interests of those mobilized to support it. Commenting on the modern age and the emergence of a mass media, Adorno believed that the modern public sphere of film, radio and, in particular, television enforces conformity, quiets dissent and mutes thought. Negative media representation has been a major factor in shaping anti-Romani sentiments and has been notable in orchestrating forms of 'moral panic' against the Roma – basically, a form of hysteria fuelled by misleading tropes and inaccurate reporting (Kroon et al, 2016). Such reporting is, in part, a product of the increase in antigypsyism being coordinated and orchestrated by unscrupulous politicians, but as authoritarian regimes and their allies take control of media outlets, this interplay in stoking moral panics has become more intense.

Anti-Romani sentiments also have an economic dynamic. Thomas Piketty (2020) argues that the growing accumulation of wealth by the top 1 per cent has led to neoliberal globalization and populism increasingly working together and/ or reflecting shared xenophobic narratives in the scapegoating of immigrants and minority ethnic groups as undermining the position of a previously incorporated (white) working class, who are now the 'left behind' as an underclass. This has been most evident in the UK referendum vote to leave the European Union (EU) in 2016 and in the election of Donald Trump as President of the US in the same year, where we can see a fusion of neoliberal competition and populist nativism. Sensationalist media reporting of mobile (migrant) EU Roma from the 'new' EU member states begging on the streets of major Western European cities and setting up camps on the outskirts were vilified by the media, and politicians used those images for political gain and as evidence of the problems brought about by uncontrolled immigration, namely, crime and abuse of social welfare.

In Central and Eastern Europe, the strengthening and growth of the radical right and nationalist regimes in countries such as Poland and Hungary, and more generally the anti-migrant hysteria that was generated by the 2015 migration of large numbers of Syrian refugees into Europe, demonstrate the growing strength of radical-right movements across Europe. The economic and financial crisis of 2008 acted as a catalyst to the rise of radical-right populism (Mudde, 2018b). A difficult economic situation, coupled with an increasingly reactive and emotive political environment, has made the position of the Roma more precarious through increased economic exclusion, scapegoating and racism (see Chapter One). Filcak and Skobla (2012) suggest that the experiences of Roma are like the 'canary in the mine shaft', that is, the harbinger of future crises. In other words, the Roma are a group that has experienced the impact of transition more harshly than others; this was very true as parts of Europe turned to fascism in the 1930s, then to communism in the post-war era, then to neoliberalism in the 1990s, and now to austerity, ordoliberalism and more entrenched forms of neoliberalism. During all these transitions, the Roma have been cast as a threat, a danger and a problem. By weakening the social contract, neoliberalism creates an 'underclass' of the unemployed and disadvantaged, a group where many Roma are to be found, and this pool also serves neoliberal interests by creating downward pressure on wages and rights in the workforce, with those in work fearing the risk of joining the ranks of the unemployed. The 'underclass' also serves as a scapegoat for those dissatisfied with the status quo to blame for their misfortunes, distracting blame from those in control. The Roma are thus cast as a socio-economic burden, a dysfunctional group prone to dependency and welfarism, committing benefit fraud, and embodying a 'culture of poverty'.

The linkages between politics, policy and practice are continually being renegotiated, and authoritarian neoliberalism certainly foregrounds welfare as socio-political governmentality through discipline, compliance and control, combined with austerity, by blaming Roma for abusing the system. Such a stance can be described as 'welfare chauvinism', an explicit and systematic marginalization of subordinate Roma (Bruff and Tansel, 2019) and/or a rationale for imposing additional conditions on Roma (Vidra, 2018).

To help illustrate such processes in context, we can look at the case of Hungary. Szombati (2018) seeks to understand the rise of antigypsyism by using Polányi's conceptualization of the 'double movement', that is, the expectation that economic shocks generated within a 'disembedded economy' will generate 'countermovements' in the political sphere if the state fails to protect society from the advance of the free market and/or from instability. For Szombati, the 2008–09 crisis was paired with the ideological orientation and political strategizing of some racist movements in Hungary (the Jobbik Party and the Magyar Garda, a radical-right paramilitary organization), developing a 'political antigypsyism' that transferred generally prevalent racist sensibilities from the social sphere into the arena of political struggle. It is worth noting the traction the Jobbik Party and the Magyar Garda generated through their 'Gypsy crime' propaganda and agitation, which claimed the Roma were predisposed to criminality and that there was a need for greater sanctioning and control of this minority. This narrative thrust the Jobbik Party forth from the political margins to becoming the largest single opposition party in the Parliament (Szombati, 2018). The various forms of demonization of Romani communities outlined here so far form the locus of a series of 'moral panics', what Cohen (2002) defines as collective hysteria (see Chapter One), and this labelling and vilification can be described as constituting antigypsyism.

Understanding antigypsyism

Having charted the causes and forms of radical-right populism and nationalism, and their impact on the Roma, this chapter proceeds to explore the response of Romani civil society to this circumstance. A major reference point of Romani civil society's counter-narrative is the concept of antigypsyism – but what is it?

One of the most prominent champions of the use of the term 'antigypsyism' is the Romanian Romani activist Valeriu Nicolae (2006: 1), who perceives antigypsyism as a distinct form of racism against Roma that is both similar to, different from and 'intertwined with many other types of racism'. It is a term that is now part of mainstream discourse about Roma and has even entered the lexicon of institutional power in Europe. The term has received growing support within the EU; in 2019, the European Parliament passed a resolution calling for the EU and its member states to adopt strong Romani inclusion plans post–2020 and to step up the fight against antigypsyism (ERGO, 2019).

The European Commission against Racism and Intolerance (ECRI) of the Council of Europe (CoE) defines antigypsyism as 'a specific form of racism, an ideology founded on racial superiority, a form of dehumanization and institutional racism nurtured by historical discrimination, which is expressed, among others, by violence, hate speech, exploitation, stigmatization and the most blatant kind of discrimination' (ECRI, 2011: 3). That definition was included in ECRI's 'General Policy Recommendation No.13 on combating anti-Gypsyism and discrimination against Roma' (ECRI, 2011). Similarities can be found between antigypsyism and antisemitism: both are persistent historically and geographically; both are systematic; and both are manifested by acts of violence. The international civil society group Alliance against Antigypsyism (2017) also argues that antigypsyism essentializes and creates discriminating social structures and violent practices that reproduce structural disadvantages.

It should be noted that there is an ongoing debate as to the appropriateness of 'antigypsyism' as a term, with Oprea and Matache (2019) arguing that it is wrong to use a term based on the word 'Gypsy', which has pejorative connotations, and that the identification of this phenomenon should instead be based on the more inclusive term 'Roma' to frame the concept of anti-Romani racism. Others use a capital 'G' in the spelling of 'anti-Gypsyism'. Reflecting on such concerns, some authors are trying to define Romani-specific forms of racism by producing new vocabularies (Albert, 2012). McGarry (2017) has employed the term 'Romaphobia' as 'the last acceptable form of racism'. I disagree with the term as 'phobia' per se relates to an 'extreme or irrational fear or aversion to something', in this case, the Roma. I contend in this chapter that antigypsyism has ideological, political and economic features that are instrumentalized through concrete policies towards Roma. Antigypsyism can be traced to historically different social, economic and political realities; it has a multifaceted character but it cannot be reduced to simply being an emotional fear on the part of the non-Roma. The term 'antigypsyism' is connected with social stereotypes, clichés and prejudices that are rather enrooted in dehumanization and the view that Roma are incompatible with 'civilized' society and fundamentally subhuman. This chapter employs the term 'antigypsyism' because, at present, it is the term accepted by most civil society stakeholders. We do not wish to enter the debate on terminology and the relevance of umbrella terms, but want to discuss the definition and application of the currently prevailing term.

It is claimed that the term 'antigypsyism' first appeared in the late 1920s in Russia, was evident in academic debates in the 1970s and 1980s, and started to feature in the narratives and 'frames' of Romani rights campaigners from the 21st century (Cortés and End, 2019). According to Goffman (1974), 'framing' offers a conceptual structure that organizes interpretation through which people understand and construct social events. Goffman's concept has provided an important source of inspiration for scholars who have studied social movements and how frames can mobilize and steer social movements. The term 'antigypsyism' has formed an important frame in the armoury of the Romani social movement. For example, it has been promoted by the Alliance against Antigypsyism (2017) – an ad hoc alliance of Romani and pro-Romani civil society organizations and individuals calling upon the EU and other power structures, such as local and national governments, to place a greater emphasis on tackling antigypsyism – and has become a prominent feature of Romani rights campaign rhetoric.

How does antigypsyism manifest itself? The expressed rhetoric of hate speech against Roma results in tacit forms of their exclusion from public services, such as access to electricity, water, sanitation and so on. Such hate speech is not just orchestrated by elites, but enters everyday language and becomes casual and accepted on social media, creating what have been described as 'micro-aggressions', namely, unthinking remarks that betray underlying assumptions and make the people targeted feel uncomfortable or violated (End, 2014). In addition, we should consider the actions taken by those in power that negatively affect Romani communities and contravene the protective function of the state towards members of the public, such as forced evictions, allowing Roma to reside only at the margins of localities, police brutality and school segregation. Furthermore, it is worth mentioning the institutional antigypsyism that has recently been recognized by the EU as one of the main barriers to Romani integration (Carrera et al, 2017). Institutional manifestations of antigypsyism have profound repercussions for the effective socio-economic inclusion of Romani communities in different life spheres, such as access to housing, health and education (FRA, 2018). What makes antigypsyism a special form of racism in Europe today is the involvement of the state in the production and co-production of these discriminatory norms, knowledge and politics in relation to Romani communities.

Racism can be defined as an ideology and a practice that produces a society in which some people systematically have less access to resources, power, security and well-being than others. Such systemic inequalities reflect hierarchical differences between people originally created by colonialism, which produced patterns of historical inequality, making it difficult for certain people to access opportunities and resources. If we accept this definition, and antigypsyism as a special form of racism, then antigypsyism clearly plays a central role in maintaining Romani marginalization in a broad socio-economic and cultural sense.

The term 'antigypsyism' could be perceived as having parallels with antisemitism, implying that specific forms of racism might exist. Anthias and Yuval Davies (1992) argue that there are 'racisms|' rather than 'racism', in other words, the experiences of racism are specific to particular groups and are historically grounded. In this sense, the term 'antigypsyism' has relevance. Mac An Ghaill (1999) has drawn attention to the plight of Gypsies, Roma and Travellers (GRT), who receive much negative media and political attention in the UK, and notes that there is a long history of neglect, both by the state and by anti-racist movements, of the material and cultural experiences of GRT communities. Thus, combating antigypsyism could become a valuable tool to challenge the marginalization of these groups through affirmative, targeted measures and mobilizations.

Transformative change and combating antigypsyism

A review of the calls for reform and change made by those who espouse the term 'antigypsyism' finds that these calls include references to improving the cultural and political representation of Roma and corresponding calls for stronger legal measures to tackle this specific form of racism. In reflecting on the value of such aspirations, it might be useful to review the conceptual debates that have taken place between the proponents of liberal multiculturalism, anti-racism and critical multiculturalism.

Liberal multiculturalism embodies a version of liberal 'tolerance' based on the assumption that there is a dominant cultural identity to which minority ethnic groups have to adapt but that concessions could be made for members of minority ethnic groups. An important aspect of liberal multiculturalism has been the belief that education and cultural promotion can dispel the ignorance that allegedly fuels racist beliefs; basically, it rests on the assumption that we can educate people not to be racist. However, critics of liberal multiculturalism claim it caricatures culture in a simplistic manner, reducing the presentation of minority cultures so as to render them homogeneous, static and internally conflict-free. Moreover, it is argued that such an approach fails to challenge the institutional dimension of racism and offers minority ethnic groups mere tokenism. Some would argue liberal multiculturalism enables forms of tokenism to act simultaneously with overt acts of institutional racism. For example, governments that include references to Roma in the school curriculum or that sponsor some form of celebration of Romani culture do so as a form of cover to enable them to profess a commitment to Romani inclusion when, in reality, they are complicit in maintaining Romani exclusion. For example, the Hungarian government has some measures to promote Romani culture in the school curriculum but is actively building an apparatus to maintain and extend school segregation (see Chapter Four by Rorke).

Proponents of anti-racism seek to challenge and dismantle the institutional components of racism in terms of the strategic direction and management of institutions, as well as the ethos and messages conveyed by them, and by promoting diversity of membership and participation in institutions. Rigid conceptions of anti-racism in the 1970s and 1980s have been criticized for relying on superficial generalizations and an over-focusing on institutional factors to the neglect of gender and class issues. Furthermore, it has been argued that anti-racism has been dependent upon rigid conceptions of racial identity that assume actors are the passive agents of homogeneous cultural identities. Proponents of the term 'antigypsyism' need to be attentive to the danger that some of the initiatives resulting from their endeavours could succumb to the deficiencies associated with liberal multiculturalism and anti-racism. The importance of the discourse, representation and epistemology of anti-racism suggests that these notions are unable to explain the complexities of the racialization process operating as part of assemblages that are impacting the Roma in everyday life (for a general overview, see Colombo, 2015).

A review of the campaign literature by the supporters of the term 'antigypsyism' indicates they do express some desire for structural change. Romani civil society has called for a strengthened rights-based approach, guided by an official working definition of antigypsyism, and has stressed the need for more ambitious targets and concrete social inclusion goals, with measurable EU and national indicators and robust annual monitoring. Within such petitions for change are demands to eradicate segregation and drive out discriminatory recruitment practices that marginalize the Roma. It is interesting to note, though, that these activists do not acknowledge the impact of the financial crisis in Europe or how neoliberalism has accentuated Romani exclusion (for further discussion, see Chapter One). This failure has clearly been a consequence of agenda-setting not only by philanthropic foundations, but by bodies like USAID, the World Bank, the International Monetary Fund (IMF) and so on, which are champions of the prevailing bias for free markets and open societies centred on neoliberalism, a state of affairs that has neglected the importance of social and economic rights. Old debates have re-emerged as to whether to privilege socio-economic inclusion over combating racism and discrimination; at this juncture, it makes sense to review Nancy Fraser's views on the politics of recognition and redistribution.

The marginalization, exclusion and demonization that ethnic groups like the Roma are subject to is based on racism, othering and the projection of stereotypes that constitutes cultural 'misrecognition', and this is compounded by 'misdistribution', or what can be termed a lack of services and resources, which further marginalizes groups like the Roma. Nancy Fraser (1995) has argued that redistribution and recognition must be united in attempts to understand and challenge social injustice. However, such a course of action may require political and transformative approaches favouring the deconstruction and destabilization of existing identities, codes and symbolic orders; in place of assimilatory (or narrow liberal multicultural) inclusion policies, new, bolder strategies may be required that empower, intervene and correct where the markets and institutions of the state hinder and impede social justice for Romani communities.

In terms of the process of mediating what social justice is and how it can be delivered, we need to consider the importance and value of representation. Fraser has noted how status hierarchies map onto class differentials to block groups like the Roma from participation in mainstream arenas of social interaction. In other words, economic, political and cultural structures work together to deny participation. This chapter argues, therefore, that definitions of antigypsyism and calls for programmes of action that stem from the term need to incorporate a more transformative agenda that offers the potential to bring about fundamental socio-economic and cultural change. Such change should be seen as a sharp contrast to remedies centred on liberal multiculturalism and the narrow social inclusion policies that have formed the mainstay of national and EU policy towards the Roma.

In forwarding transformative change as an aim of the Romani social movement, proponents of the term 'antigypsyism' may need to be sensitive to the potential insularity among Roma that can arise from using the term. In this respect, it is worthwhile reviewing some of the critique of the concept of antisemitism, where some observers feel there is a disconnection between racism and antisemitism, as reflected in the intellectual specialization and separate development of postcolonial and Holocaust studies that, while having nurtured fruitful research in their respective fields, may have constructed disconnected frames of analysis, and even antagonism, between Black minority groups and Jewish social actors. Such fissures are evident in contemporary academic discourses, such as those on 'critical race theories' and 'new antisemitism' theories. Both of these conceptual frames seek to recognize and resist 'new' forms of racism and antisemitism, and have drawn attention to covert and subtle forms of prejudice; conversely, it is said they have a tendency to see racism and antisemitism as exclusive and ubiquitous (Cousin and Fine, 2012). It could be argued, though, that the proponents of antigypsyism may be able to escape charges of insularity through the growing commitment of young leaders in the Romani social movement to intersectionality, to the value of alliances between different minority groups and to the exploration of shared experiences of exclusion and marginality across groups. Such alliances, it is argued, can help create a patchwork quilt of a broad social movement based on strategic alliances between a range of minority groups.

Intersectionality is an important component of critical multiculturalism, which seeks to explore the interplay between race, gender, class, sexual identity and oppressive behaviours and practices (Farrar, 2012). It encompasses anti-racist education, critical race theory and critical pedagogy, which challenge the social, economic and cultural drivers of exclusion and xenophobia. It is a more intercultural and deliberative form of identity management which recognizes that identity is neither rigid nor static, and that change and innovation are both possible and to be welcomed. It can be described as a more dialogic and negotiable form of multiculturalism that challenges oppressive outlooks in both majority and minority society. In such discussion, reference can be made to Parekh's (2000) notion of cultivating a 'sense of common belonging' among citizens that requires no flattening of diversity and allows for plurality.

Perhaps most importantly with reference to antigypsyism, critical multiculturalism has the potential to understand and challenge white privilege and thus the structural factors that divide ethnic groups and the cultural perceptions that reinforce and justify such divides. Such a form of challenge would give antigypsyism, as a transformative tool, the scope and conceptual power to more effectively offer resistance to the cultural and socio-economic hegemony that marginalizes Romani communities. The Roma have clearly not been passive victims and are offering creative responses to the dilemma they face; in part, this is attributable to what can be termed 'social resilience': the ability to cope with and overcome adversity through adaptation learnt from past experiences, and to adjust themselves to future challenges. This has transformative potential in devising counter-strategies and solutions. A key factor in forming resistance to marginalization has been a sense of pride in Romani ethnicity (McGarry, 2017). The value of pride cannot be underestimated; Nicolae (2006) notes that antigypsyist messages can and are absorbed and accepted by Roma in the form of false consciousness, leading to the desire to assimilate and to self-stigmatization, depression and demoralization. In the past, though, pride in Romani identity, while socially bonding, could also create insularity and isolation. New forms of Romani pride that encompass intersectional and critical forms of multiculturalism will be invaluable in promoting intercultural dialogue and new strategic alliances with other oppressed communities. Such fluidity and the reinvention and adaptation of identity mirrors what the renowned sociologist Stuart Hall (1980) has explained, namely, how ethnic identity could enable a new cultural politics to emerge, one that engages rather than suppresses difference and is capable of challenging Western white cultural hegemony.

An attempt to challenge stereotypical representations of the Roma and give expression to new articulations of Romani identity is evidenced by the establishment of the European Roma Institute for Arts and Culture (ERIAC), based in Berlin and funded jointly by the Council of Europe and EU, with support from the philanthropist George Soros. ERIAC has given a platform to a range of avant-garde Romani artists and musicians positing new, dynamic conceptions of Romani identity that challenge tradition and reification. Critics of ERIAC, however, argue that there is a danger of such a project tokenizing the language of critical challenge and empowerment while actually being 'highbrow' and focused on a small intellectual elite among European Roma (Ryder, 2019). Time will tell whether this initiative is capable of energizing Romani arts and culture initiatives within local Romani communities and society more widely in a way that challenges long-standing tropes and prejudices.

Laclau and Mouffe (2001) support grass-roots politics, building on the ideas of Gramsci and the frames of new social movements centred on intersectional notions of gender, sexuality, ethnicity and economic justice. In this sense, the notion of 'Social Europe' and a greater emphasis on redistribution, coupled with recognition, could strengthen Romani civil society in making alliances not just with other minority groups, but with social movements dedicated to raising social justice, such as the trade union movement when in a transformative form. Some of the more liberal, rights-focused Romani activists might feel apprehensive about such alliances and a transformative agenda, fearing this might alienate some elements of establishment support and might overtly politicize the Romani issue. Policy positions, though, are relative; positions and stances that might seem radical and utopian today were part of the political mainstream in many countries five decades ago.

What the French economist Jean Fourastié (1979) termed 'Les trente glorieuses' ('the 30 glorious years'), in retrospect is seen as a gilded age where living standards rose dramatically from 1945 to 1975. The 'glorious thirty' saw large parts of the developed world commit to strong forms of social contract, with the development of universal and comprehensive welfare systems and a commitment to full employment guided by Keynesian economics. Post-war society learnt from the failure of laissez-faire economics during the deeply troubled 1930s, and from the rise of fascism, that the best antidote to extremism was economic stability, fairness and a human rights framework, principles that advocates of a New Social Europe believe we need to relearn.

The advent of neoliberalism unbalanced this consensus and the gradualist trajectory of reform and social progression. Nationalism and authoritarian populism have sought to fill the emerging vacuum with pledges to upend the status quo in the name of fairness. Parties of the centre-left have been ill-equipped to harness growing popular frustrations given their alignment with the neoliberal order through 'Third Way' politics. However, proponents of a Social Europe agenda are not advocating the return to post-war statism, for despite their commitments to social justice, such regimes were hierarchical, bureaucratic and paternalistic. A New Social Europe would be guided by civil society (for a definition of civil society, see Chapter One).

In the present day, some hold the fear that civil society is being increasingly tamed and subverted by the state and donors. To use a term of the new right, 'pulling back the state' has been accompanied by a series of governmental strategies and technologies (governmentality) that, through top-down stipulations being attached to funding and overt promotion of the donor's agenda, weaken the autonomy of civil society (van Baar, 2011a). Policies that invoke the language of social inclusion rest upon narrow, assimilative interpretations of what it is to 'civilize' and integrate others. Vibrant grass-roots activism among Romani communities and other communities could create a new policy regime predicated upon radical conceptions of inclusion. In effect, rather than civil society being a puppet of the state, it would be transformed into a key partner and a guide for government. Inclusive community development that builds on and develops existing skills and cultural practices, and that is community-driven, can be an important dynamic in creating an inclusive policy framework. In a process of 'reverse governmentality', rather than government using civil society as a tool to impose narrow inclusion/assimilation policies, we would instead see a situation where civil society takes leadership, demands proportional representation in politics and increases the public space for self-determination to give concrete expression to the emancipatory potential within Romani communities (Ryder and Taba, 2018). This point reiterates a central argument of this volume, namely, that an effective Social Europe approach for Romani communities requires greater support for the development and expansion of Romani civil society in a manner that extends not just its capacity and skills, but also its autonomy.

In this sense, Romani civil society could constitute part of what Fraser (1992) described as a subaltern public sphere, where, through forms of collectivity and social enterprise, mini public forums would be created that would be useful in the formulation of counter-narratives, especially for marginalized groups who are poorly represented in the formal world of politics. In this sense, civil society has the potential to offer what Laclau and Mouffe (2001) describe as 'chains of equivalence', where marginalized groups can ally themselves behind their common opposition to forms of oppression but each retain a different logic and their own particular political identities and strategies. In this sense, if definitions of antigypsyism place greater emphasis on giving the Roma agency and a voice, it could do much to challenge the image of Roma as incapable of leadership in the body politic through their lack of skills or alleged cultural inclinations, and instead could emphasize the potential of Romani capabilities and the emancipatory potential within Romani communities.

With the rise of radical-right populism, we should not forget that there is, as noted earlier, a form of leftist populism, also steered by agonism and its own conception of the 'will of the people' and 'us and them', centred on economic elites. The French anthropologist and sociologist Fassin has criticized leftist populism, claiming it is fuelled by resentment, which ultimately, as with nationalist populism, cannot be immune to reaction and scapegoating (Hamburger, 2018).

The German philosopher Habermas has sought to revive notions of consensus based on deliberation within liberal politics; his writings also contain a corresponding commitment to social justice through his calls to challenge capitalism. Deliberative politics, it could be argued, has an important advantage over agonism in an age when politics seems to be increasingly characterized by fissure and dissension as it does not provoke and mobilize the support base of the adversary through dogmatic polemic. Instead, through dialogue, reinterpretation and reorientation, deliberative politics seeks to dilute the views of its adversaries and convert them. The challenge, though, is to achieve such a state of affairs without recourse to the anodyne politics of the neoliberal Washington Consensus, the period that preceded the 'glorious thirty' or other such appeasement (Ryder, 2020).

A New Social Europe could offer solutions that would also appeal to the constituencies of opinion that have mobilized in support of radical-right populism, especially in deindustrialized and 'left behind' communities. Such communities might be persuaded to reorient their political aspirations if promised a version of the 'good society' that would entail transformative, interventionist, redistributive policies with the ability to create work and rebuild communities. This could be part of a counter-narrative to the politics of nativism, xenophobia and nationalism. A Habermasian vision of deliberative politics could entail accommodations in matters that eschew violence and hostility, and defuse tension. However, there will always be moments of antagonism, and irreconcilable claims will always surface, especially from those who wield unaccountable power, wealth and undemocratic influence. In between elections, the mass of the citizenry should be voluntarily engaged, through a vibrant civil society, to participate, to get involved and to feel they really belong to the *demos*, a bounded political community of fate, in ways that are consistent with cosmopolitan obligation and do not exclude others from meaningful participation and representation on any spurious grounds of ethnicity, gender, ability, faith and so on.

The Habermasian tradition of deliberation and dialogue would not shy away from forms of conflict resolution, even when negotiating with adversaries aligned to the Right, so long as core principles and values are not compromised. To gain insights into the application of such strategies in the Romani sphere, we could refer to the work of the greatly acclaimed Nicolae Gheorghe, who, while leader of the Romani NGO Roma Centre for Social Intervention and Studies (Romani

CRISS) in Romania, was active in conflict resolution. Gheorghe's work centred on dialogue and negotiation in communities where extreme ethnic tensions and pogroms had flared up, which sometimes entailed dialogue with those holding deeply ingrained anti-Romani sentiments. It is interesting to note that lead proponents of the term 'antigypsyism', such as the former MEP Soraya Post, who is of Romani origin, have called for a truth and reconciliation process about the history of the Roma in Europe, noting such initiatives in South Africa, Canada and Australia with indigenous groups, and, most recently, in Sweden, which led to Roma being recognized as a national minority there (LIBE, 2019). Such initiatives, it could be argued, have more to do with Habermasian deliberative politics than with leftist agonism, and it is useful that a framework for antigypsyism as a political tool incorporates and sanctions such dialogue. What this chapter has striven to emphasize, though, is that deliberation, reconciliation and cultural promotion will have limited value as stand-alone policies if not coupled with the transformative change promised through a New Social Europe.

Habermas provides another point of inspiration for Romani civil society in his discussion of the public sphere. Habermas (1989) defines the public sphere as a public network that shapes opinion through frames (viewpoints). Under advanced capitalism, Habermas posits that the discursive power of the public sphere has been emasculated through its colonization by the state and the market, where standardized mass media has erased the capacity for critical thought and manipulated it to create a notion of consensus geared to the interests of elites. Thus, the populace is swayed by the communicative techniques of advertising and marketing, creating unthinking citizens, a form of 're-feudalization' that limits the public's capacity for critical thinking. As noted earlier, the media has been a powerful force in the politics of securitization and anxiety, and in the instigation of moral panics against the Roma. Hence, the

Romani rights defenders ranged against antigypsyism should incorporate more detailed proposals to reform the media into their calls for action, such as stronger ethical codes for journalism, stronger fines and penalties, and a right to reply in the event of distorted reporting, as well as limitations on the number of media outlets any individual can own. In terms of wider legal protections for the Roma, maintaining the rule of law is paramount – a notion that is invariably undermined and challenged by the radical right; in this sense, the proposal for a rule of law mechanism to scrutinize EU member state practices and violations has great merit (LIBE, 2019). However, austerity has greatly eroded legal aid schemes in many EU member states, so improved funding in this area and more community-based paralegals could be invaluable in giving Roma greater legal redress to challenge antigypsyism. More generally, greater resources and access to the machinery of justice is needed to ensure Romani rights are protected.

Conclusion

We live in an age of crisis and turmoil, as evidenced by the rise of authoritarian populism and nationalism. Nonetheless, this chapter has argued that transformative notions of antigypsyism could have value at this time. The term 'antigypsyism' could have utility and relevance if aligned with critical thinking, with radical forms of empowerment that reach the margins, with challenges to white hegemony and the neoliberal order, with the promotion of fluid conceptions of identity, and with a commitment to a radical deliberative politics and alliance building centred on intersectionality and social justice. Romani civil society should be vigilant, for there is a danger that institutional power might merely accept the softer forms of action associated with the term 'antigypsyism' and neglect the more structural, transformative change required to address the marginalization of the Roma.

References

Adorno, T.W. (1948) 'Remarks on the authoritarian personality', Max Horkheimer archive, Universitätsbibliothek, Goethe Universität, http://sammlungen.ub.uni-frankfurt.de/horkheimer/content/zoom/6323018?zoom=1&lat=1600&lon=1000&layers=B

Adorno, T.W., Frenkel-Brunswik, E., Levinson, D.J. and Sanford, R.N. (1950) *The Authoritarian Personality*, New York, NY: Harper & Row.

Albert, G. (2012) 'Anti-Gypsyism and the extreme-right in the Czech Republic', in M. Stewart (ed) *The Gypsy 'Menace': Populism and the New Anti-Gypsy Politics*, London: Hurst and Company, pp 137–66.

Alliance against Antigypsyism (2017) 'A reference paper on antigypsyism', https://www.antigypsyism.eu/?page_id=17

Amnesty International (2020) 'Stigmatizing quarantines of Roma settlements in Slovakia and Bulgaria', www.amnesty.org/download/Documents/EUR0121562020ENGLISH.PDF

Anthias, F. and Yuval Davis, N. (1992) *Racialised Boundaries*, London: Routledge.

Bruff, I. and Tansel, C. (2019) 'Authoritarian neoliberalism: Trajectories of knowledge production and praxis', *Globalizations*, 16(3): 233–44.

Carrera, S., Rostas, I. and Vosyliūtė, L. (2017) 'Combating institutional anti-Gypsyism: Responses and promising practices in the EU and selected Member States', www.ceps.eu/system/files/RR2017-08_AntiGypsyism.pdf

Cohen, P. (2002) *Folk Devils and Moral Panics* (3rd edn), London: Routledge.

Colombo, E. (2015) 'Multiculturalisms: An overview of multicultural debates in Western societies', *Current Sociology*, 63(6): 800–24.

Cortés, G.I. and End, M. (2019) 'Dimensions of antigypsyism in Europe', European Network Against Racism, www.enar-eu.org/Book-Dimensions-of-Antigypsyism-in-Europe

Cousin, G. and Fine, R. (2012) 'A common cause', *European Societies*, 14(2): 166–85.

Dryzek, J.S. and Niemeyer, S. (2006) 'Reconciling pluralism and consensus as political ideals', *American Journal of Political Science*, 50: 634–49.

ECRI (The European Commission against Racism and Intolerance) (2011) *General Policy Recommendation no.13 on Combatting Anti-Gypsyism and Discrimination against Roma*, Strasbourg: ECRI https://rm.coe.int/ecri-general-policy-recommendation-no-13-on-combating-anti-gypsyism-an/16808b5aee

Edwards, J. (2013) 'Play and democracy: Huizinga and the limits of agonism', *Political Theory*, 41(1): 90–115.

End, M. (2014) 'Antiziganism as a structure of meanings: The racial antiziganism of an Austrian Nazi', in T. Agarin (ed) *When Stereotype Meets Prejudice: Antiziganism in European Societies*, Stuttgart: ibidem, pp 77–92.

ERGO (European Roma Grassroots Organisations) (2019) 'Strong European Parliament call to address antigypsyism', http://ergonetwork.org/2019/02/strong-european-parliament-call-to-address-antigypsyism/

Farrar, M. (2012) '"Interculturalism" or "critical multiculturalism": Which discourse works best?', in M. Farrar (ed) *Debating Multiculturalism*, London: The Dialogue Society.

Filcak, R. and Skobla, D. (2012) 'Social solidarity, human rights and Roma: Unequal access to basic resources in reinventing social solidarity across Europe', in M. Ellison (ed) *Reinventing Social Solidarity across Europe*, Bristol: Policy Press, pp 227–50.

Fourastié, J. (1979) *Les Trente Glorieuses, ou la révolution invisible de 1946 à 1975*, Paris: Fayard.

FRA (EU Agency for Fundamental Rights) 'A persisting concern: Anti-Gypsyism as a barrier to Roma inclusion', Luxembourg: Publications Office of the European Union, https://fra.europa.eu/sites/default/files/fra_uploads/fra-2018-anti-gypsyism-barrier-roma-inclusion_en.pdf

Fraser, N. (1992) 'Rethinking the public sphere: A contribution to the critique of actually existing democracy', in C. Calhoun (ed) *Habermas and the Public Sphere*, Cambridge, MA: MIT Press, pp 109–42.

Fraser, N. (1995) 'From redistribution to recognition? Dilemmas of justice in a "post-socialist" age', https://newleftreview.org/issues/I212/articles/nancy-fraser-from-redistribution-to-recognition-dilemmas-of-justice-in-a-post-socialist-age

Goffman, E. (1974) *Frame Analysis: An Essay on the Organization of Experience*, Cambridge, MA: Harvard University Press.

Habermas, J. (1989) *The Structural Transformation of the Public Sphere: An Inquiry into a Category of Bourgeois Society*, Cambridge, MA: Thomas Burger.

Hall, S. (1980) 'Popular-democratic versus authoritarian populism', in A. Hunt (ed) *Marxism and Democracy*, London: Laurence and Wishhart, pp. 157–85.

Hamburger, C. (2018) 'Can there be a left populism?', *Jacobin*, www.jacobinmag.com/2018/03/left-populism-mouffe-fassin-france-insoumise

Kroon, A.C., Kluknavská, A., Vliegenthart, R. and Boomgaarden, H.G. (2016) 'Victims or perpetrators? Explaining media framing of Roma across Europe', *European Journal of Communication*, 31(4): 375–92.

Laclau, E. and Mouffe, C. (2001) *Hegemony and Socialist Strategy: Towards a Radical Democratic Politics*, London: Verso.

LIBE (Committee on Civil Liberties, Justice and Home Affairs) (2019) 'Scaling up Roma Inclusion Strategies: Truth, reconciliation and justice for addressing antigypsyism', www.europarl.europa.eu/RegData/etudes/STUD/2019/608859/IPOL_STU(2019)608859_EN.pdf

Mac an Ghaill, M. (1999) *Contemporary Racisms and Ethnicities, Social and Cultural Transformations*, Buckingham, PA: Open University Press.

McGarry, A. (2017) *Romophobia: The Last Acceptable Form of Racism*, London: Zed Books.

Monbiot, G. (2019) 'Performative oppression', *The Guardian*, 13 November, www.monbiot.com/2019/11/15/performative-oppression/

Mudde, C. (2007) *Populist Radical Right Parties in Europe*, Cambridge: Cambridge University Press.

Mudde, C. (2018a) 'Politics at the fringes? Eastern Europe's populists, racists, and extremists', in A. Fagan and P. Kopecky (eds) *The Routledge Handbook of East European Politics*, London and New York, NY: Routledge, p 260.

Mudde, C. (2018b) 'How populism became the concept that defines our age', *The Guardian*, 22 November, www.theguardian.com/commentisfree/2018/nov/22/populism-concept-defines-our-age

Mudde, C. and Kaltwasser, C.R. (2017) *Populism: A Very Short Introduction*, Oxford: Oxford University Press.

Nicolae, V. (2006) 'Towards a definition of anti-Gypsyism', http://ergonetwork.org/wp-content/uploads/2019/01/Valeriu-Nicholae_towards-a-definition-of-antigypsyism.pdf

Oprea, A. and Matache, M. (2019) 'Reclaiming the narrative: A critical assessment of terminology in the fight for Roma rights', in G. Cortés and M. End, 'Dimensions of antigypsyism in Europe 2019', European Network Against Racism, www.enar-eu.org/Book-Dimensions-of-Antigypsyism-in-Europe

Parekh, B. (2000) *The Report of the Commission on the Future of Multi-Ethnic Britain*, London: Profile Books.

Parker, O. (2012) Roma and the politics of EU citizenship in France: Everyday security and resistance', *Journal of Common Market Studies*, 50(3): 475–91.

Piketty, T. (2020) *Capital and Ideology*, Cambridge: Belknap Press.

Polanyi, K. (1944) *The Great Transformation* (Foreword by R.M. MacIver), New York, NY: Farrar & Rinehart.

Roskamm, N. (2015) 'On the other side of "agonism": "The enemy," the "outside," and the role of antagonism', *Planning Theory*, 14(4): 384–403.

Ryder, A. (2019) 'A game of thrones: Power struggles and contestation in Romani studies', https://hipatiapress.com/hpjournals/index.php/ijrs/article/view/4197

Ryder, A. (2020) *Britain and Europe at the Crossroads: The Politics of Anxiety and Transformation*, Bristol: Policy Press.

Ryder, A. and Taba, M. (2018) 'Roma and Social Europe', *The Journal of Poverty and Social Justice*, 17(special edition: 'Roma in a Time of Paradigm Shift and Chaos'): 59–75.

Santayana, G. (2006) *The Life of Reason: Five Volumes in One*, Cirencester: Echo Library.

Schmitt, S. (1996) *The Concept of the Political* (trans G. Schwab), Chicago, IL: University of Chicago Press.

Szombati, K. (2018) *The Revolt of the Provinces Anti-Gypsyism and Right-Wing Politics in Hungary*, New York, NY: Berghahn Books.

van Baar, H. (2011a) 'The European Roma: Minority representation, memory, and the limits of transnational governmentality', PhD thesis, Amsterdam School for Cultural Analysis.

van Baar, H. (2011b) 'Commentary: Europe's Romaphobia: Problematization, securitization, nomadization', *Environment and Planning D: Society and Space*, 29: 203–12.

Vidra, Z. (2018) 'Hungary's punitive turn: The shift from welfare to workfare', *Communist and Post-Communist Studies*, 15(1): 73–80.

FOUR

Antigypsyism in Hungary: the Gyöngyöspata case versus 'the people's sense of justice'

Bernard Rorke

Introduction

In the ten years since Viktor Orbán's 'revolution in the polling booths' delivered Fidesz an unprecedented two-thirds majority, and established a 'new regime of national unity' (Dunai and Than, 2010), Hungary's Romani community has found itself constantly targeted by a broad constituency of far-right politicians and pundits. One consequence of the consolidation of authoritarian nativist rule in Hungary and the regime's constant aggressive xenophobia has been the effective mainstreaming of antigypsyism. Nonetheless, the prime minister's intervention in the recent Gyöngyöspata case marked an unprecedented escalation. Chapter Three in this volume by Marius Taba charted the rise of the radical right in Europe, and how nativist demagogues seem to have taken their cue from the Carl Schmitt playbook by peddling an antagonistic friend–enemy concept of the political, and a polarizing, exclusivist notion of the nation that frequently deploys anti-Romani racism. This short chapter provides insights into one such process.

I argue that in its perpetual Schmittian search for an enemy in a state of exception, the Orbán regime in Hungary made a calculated decision to turn its fire on the Roma. Stung by its partial defeat in the 2019 municipal elections (Kovács, 2019), especially the loss of Budapest, which deflated the illusion of regime invincibility, Fidesz lurched even further to the right. The diminishing returns from demonizing Muslims, migrants and refugees prompted Orbán and his propagandists to revive an older hatred and weaponize antigypsyism.

The pretext was a four-month-old court ruling by the Debrecen Court of Appeal in favour of Romani families in the town of Gyöngyöspata whose children were forced to learn in segregated settings between 2004 and 2014. On 18 September 2019, the Debrecen Court of Appeal upheld the first instance judgment of Eger Regional Court and concluded that the Hungarian state was required to pay HUF80 million (£205,382) in compensation to Romani children who had been segregated for a decade from their peers in school. Seemingly out of the blue, Orbán described this decision as having violated 'the people's sense of justice'. Before recounting what occurred after this first prime ministerial intervention into the Gyöngyöspata case, the next section provides some context concerning the school segregation and desegregation of Romani pupils in Hungary over the past decade.

A brief history of school segregation

Immediately prior to the launch of the Decade of Roma Inclusion in 2005, the European Roma Rights Centre (ERRC) reported to the European Commission that the 'recent legal and policy amendments aiming to combat racial segregation in schooling in Hungary' were 'among the most far-reaching and innovative policies on Roma anywhere in Europe' (Rorke, 2015).

However, by late 2010, some months after Fidesz came to power, the Hungarian Civil Liberties Union reported that efforts to integrate Romani children and introduce innovative pedagogic methods into the educational system had come to a halt, and that the government had started to question 'the hegemony of an integrated system' (Rorke, 2015). What followed was that a national commitment to school desegregation came to be displaced by a cynical policy of 'separate but equal'-style segregation, repackaged as 'social catching up'.

In 2013, in the case of *Horváth and Kiss v. Hungary*, the European Court of Human Rights ruled that the two Romani applicants who were diagnosed as having mild mental disabilities as children and were placed in remedial school suffered indirect ethnic discrimination. Furthermore, the Court insisted that the state has a substantive positive obligation to 'undo a history of racial segregation' (Timmer, 2013).

November 2014 saw Minister for Human Resources Zoltán Balog file a Bill to amend Hungary's Public Education Act 2011 to effectively legalize school segregation (Tóth, 2014) following a court decision in a case filed by the Chance for Children Foundation (CFCF), which ordered the closure of a segregated school in Nyíregyháza run by the Greek Catholic Church. The amendment circumvented legal verdicts by exempting some schools from the requirements of the Equal Opportunities Act. Opposition MP Tímea Szabó called the modification of the law a disgrace and declared that Balog's idea of 'benevolent segregation' was contrary to both the statutes of Hungary and the European Union (EU) (Rorke, 2015).

The amendment would prove unnecessary following the subsequent decision of Hungary's Supreme Court (the *Kuria*) in April 2015 to overturn the earlier ruling and exempt the Greek Catholic Church from anti-discrimination provisions in law. This judgment effectively declared the segregation of Romani pupils legal in religious-run schools, and was memorably described by CFCF board member Gábor Daróczi as 'apartheid under the aegis of religious freedom' (Hungarian Spectrum, 2015).

In its June 2015 communication on the implementation of the EU Framework for National Roma Integration Strategies, the European Commission (2015) called for an end to school segregation and noted that Hungary counts 45 per cent of Romani children being placed in segregated schools or classes, one of the highest percentages among EU member states. On 26 May 2016, the European Commission launched an infringement procedure into systemic discrimination against Romani children in Hungary. In response, the government accused the EU of 'getting revenge' because Hungary had earlier contested the EU decision on mandatory refugee quotas, and described the procedure as 'absurd'.

The EU's *Education and Training Monitor 2018: Hungary* (European Commission, 2018) revealed a system that had become even more segregated and more unequal. The report found that early school leaving was more than six times higher (59.9 per cent) among Roma than among non-Roma (8.9 per cent), and that segregation had 'accelerated' in the last decade to the extent that 'most Roma children still attend schools where all or most children are Roma' (European Commission, 2018).

In short, evidence, research and court judgments over the past decade show that there was nothing incidental or accidental about the practices that have perpetuated segregation and inequality. Denying Hungarian Romani children equal access to integrated quality education is a deliberate, knowing and systemic practice.

'The people's sense of justice has been wounded': undermining the rule of law

Four months after the Debrecen Court of Appeal reached its decision that the state should compensate the Gyöngyöspata Romani families, Orbán suddenly picked up on the issue. In a succession of provocative broadcasts to the nation, he stated that the Court's decision 'violated the people's sense of justice', stigmatized the local Roma as workshy and their children as violent, unruly and uneducable, and asserted that what went on in Gyöngyöspata was not segregation, but 'catching up' (MTI-Hungary Today, 2020).

For their part, the Romani children testified that: they rarely met their non-Romani peers as they were educated in separate classes on a separate floor; they were not allowed to take part in the carnival ball; they were not taken on class trips; and they were denied information technology (IT) and swimming lessons. The reality of segregation was that many children were unable to graduate, and so poor was the quality of education that many barely learned to read or write (Szurovecz, 2020).

In a move favoured by white supremacists worldwide, Orbán (Miniszterelnöki Kabinetiroda, 2020) portrayed the majority ethnic group as the victims: 'Non-Roma in Gyöngyöspáta began to feel that they had to back down and apologize, despite being the majority. They feel like they are in a hostile environment in their own homeland.' The Prime Minister further opined:

> I am not from Gyöngyöspáta, but if I were to live there, I would be asking how it is that, for some reason, members of an ethnically determined group living in a community with me, in a village, can receive significant sums of money without doing any work, while I work my butt off every day. (Bayer, 2020)

Dismissing 'the whole thing as a provocation', fomented by Soros organizations, Orbán (Cseresnyés, 2020) stated that 'there is a boundary that a Hungarian will never cross, or believes cannot be crossed. That boundary is giving people money for nothing.'

Forging a robust social mandate for racism

Pro-government media further polarized opinion, with anchors, columnists and other assorted hacks queuing up to back the leader and stigmatize the Gyöngyöspata Roma. The far-right Hír TV reported that 97 per cent of viewers who responded to a poll backed Orbán on the issue (Rorke, 2020). The question Hír TV asked in the ad hoc poll was predictably loaded: 'Do you agree with Viktor Orbán, who says it is unjust that some people be paid millions without any work or with the Soros-backed organization which advocates for Roma people in Gyöngyöspata to receive a 100 million [forints] in compensation for segregation?' (Hungarian Spectrum, 2020a). Orbán then announced a new 'national consultation' on the Gyöngyöspata case, and declared 'we take the side of the 80 percent who are decent, working Hungarians who demand a suitable education for their child' (Gulyás, 2020). The national consultation is nothing more than a blatant manoeuvre to invoke the will of the people to influence the deliberations and decision of the Supreme Court on this issue. The issue is further skewed by being sandwiched between two other questions on 'the rights of violent criminals' and judicial corruption. Over the last ten years, the regime has repeatedly resorted to national consultations as part of propaganda campaigns against imagined enemies of the nation. Orbán characterizes the consultations, with their leading and loaded questions, as 'demonstrating the power of national consensus' (Gulyás, 2020). As to the outcome, the government stated that it already has clear answers to questions that have provoked social debates; 'however, it needs a robust social mandate in order to represent them in the international arena as well as within Hungary' (Gulyás, 2020).

Intimidating and stigmatizing the Roma of Gyöngyöspata

This is not the first time that the Roma of Gyöngyöspata have been targeted by the far-right. Back in 2011, uniformed neo-fascist paramilitaries, backed up by skinhead auxiliaries with whips, axes and fighting dogs, set up checkpoints and patrolled the Romani neighbourhood with seeming impunity, as policemen stood by, in a siege that lasted almost two months. As *The Guardian* reported, militiamen 'roamed the streets day and night, singing, hammering on doors and calling the inhabitants "dirty fucking Gypsies"' (Pidd, 2012). Back then, Orbán stood accused of failing to protect Romani citizens from arbitrary force and intimidation.

Now, in 2020, it is the Prime Minister who is the direct source of racially motivated intimidation. On orders from Budapest, local Fidesz MP László Horváth began campaigning against the verdict and 'the Soros network's goal to obtain money'. In language that amounts to incitement, Horváth (Hungarian Spectrum, 2020b) predicted that the discord in the village 'will lead to a nationwide storm' and declared that 'Every time strangers come to Gyöngyöspata from far-away places to fight for justice, war follows.'

'Schmittian shenanigans' would be a pithy characterization of what has unfolded here, and even more apt in light of subsequent developments. The whole package is there: the plainly daft evocation of war; a concept of the political that rests on a friend–enemy distinction, brooking no dissent when it comes to collective will-formation; and a sovereign who decides on the exception. Orbán's constant invocation of 'the authentic people', decent fair-minded Hungarians, is textbook nativism, especially when he presents them as pitted against the 'ethnically determined group', the feckless work-shy Roma, aided and abetted by foreign-funded, money-grubbing, shyster lawyers.

Orbán has further posited that there is no cultural identity in a population without a stable ethnic composition, and that economic prosperity depends on preserving ethnic homogeneity 'as life has proven that too much mixing causes trouble' (EURACTIV, 2017). Little wonder that the authors of a recent United Nations (UN) report (UNCERD, 2019), which expressed 'high concern' at the persistence of structural discrimination against, segregation of and extreme poverty faced by Roma, were 'deeply alarmed' at the prevalence of hate speech against Roma, migrants, refugees and other minority groups, as well as 'reports that public figures in the State party, including at the highest levels have made statements that may promote racial hatred'. In reaction to what he described as Orban's 'increasingly delusional' racist rhetoric, the UN High Commissioner for Human Rights was moved to declare that 'the increasingly authoritarian – though democratically elected – Viktor Orbán is a racist and xenophobe' (Al-Hussein, 2018).

The 'Gyöngyöspata case' marked the moment when the Prime Minister turned his fire from migrants onto Roma. Orbán's assertion that 'the people's sense of justice has been wounded', and that 'we need to give justice to the Gyöngyöspata people', clearly excludes the Roma from the body of 'the people'. This message was not lost on the thousands of Roma who turned out to protest against the proposed national consultation.

Then, just as opposition momentum was gathering, the pandemic hit and lockdowns kicked in all over the world. Under cover of COVID-19, the Hungarian Parliament approved a so-called enabling act on 30 March, which let Orban rule by decree without any time limit, and included a ban on elections and referenda. Regime claims that these extraordinary measures were somehow unexceptional in the time of the virus were met with incredulity and condemnation abroad; the European Parliament issued a statement describing the new measures as 'incompatible with European values' (Radio Free Europe/ Radio Liberty, 2020).

In an attempt to wrongfoot its critics, at the end of May, the government announced its intent to revoke the state of emergency decree; but as Human Rights Watch and many legal scholars have pointed out, the Revocation Bill is yet another political sleight-of-hand, for it does not revoke anything, 'but rather double-downs on Orban's power grab' (Gall, 2020).

In the midst of all these shenanigans around the state of exception, on 17 May, the Supreme Court delivered its ruling in favour of the children and parents of Gyöngyöspata, much to the fury of Orbán, who described the judgment as unfair. He said the government would decide how to honour the court ruling and was preparing new legislation to prevent any future such decisions. On national radio, Orbán launched into a chilling tirade against minorities, asking whether Hungarians can feel at home in their own country:

> It cannot happen that in order for a minority to feel at home, the majority must feel like strangers in their own towns, villages, or homeland. This is not acceptable. And as long as I am the prime minister, nothing of the sort will happen. Because this is the country of the natives, our country, and I see that this whole [Roma court] case was initiated by the Soros organizations. (Mák, 2020)

This nativist rhetoric resonates with right-wing extremists, whose *squadristi* have already recently massed on the streets in anti-Roma rallies. Observers are acutely aware that the new powers assumed by Orbán provide scope aplenty for this vengeful autocrat to settle scores, and it's only a matter of time before Roma find themselves once again in the regime's crosshairs.

References

Al-Hussein, Z.R.Z. (2018) 'Hungary: Opinion editorial by UN High Commissioner for Human Rights', OHCHR, Geneva, 6 March, www.ohchr.org/EN/NewsEvents/Pages/DisplayNews. aspx?NewsID=22765&LangID=E

Bayer, L. (2020) 'Orbán under fire over school segregation comments: Hungarian PM "crossed every moral line," says rights activist', *Politico*, 10 Januarywww.politico.eu/article/ viktor-orban-under-fire-over-school-segregation-comments/

Cseresnyés, P. (2020) 'Gov't finds court ruling on school segregation of Romas "unfortunate", refuses to pay compensation', *Hungary Today*, 20 January, https://hungarytoday.hu/govt-finds-court-ruling-on-school-segregation-of-romas-unfortunate-refuses-to-pay-compensation/

Dunai, M. and Than, K. (2010) 'Hungary's Fidesz wins historic two-thirds mandate', *Reuters*, 25 April, www.reuters.com/article/us-hungary-election/hungarys-fidesz-wins-historic-two-thirds-mandate-idUSTRE63O1KB20100425

ERRC (European Roma Rights Centre) (2013) 'Case file: Horváth and Kiss V Hungary', 29 January, www.errc.org/cikk.php?cikk=4200

EURACTIV (2017) 'Orbán calls "ethnic homogeneity" a key to success', 1 March, https://www.euractiv.com/section/justice-home-affairs/news/orban-calls-ethnic-homogeneity-a-key-to-success/

European Commission (2015) 'Communication from the Commission to the European Parliament, the Council, the European Economic and Social Committee and the Committee of the Regions: Report on the implementation of the EU Framework for National Roma Integration Strategies', Brussels, 17 June, https://ec.europa.eu/transparency/regdoc/rep/1/2015/EN/1-2015-299-EN-F1-1.PDF

European Commission (2018) *Education and Training Monitor 2018: Hungary*, Luxembourg: Publications Office of the European Union, https://ec.europa.eu/education/sites/education/files/document-library-docs/et-monitor-report-2018-hungary_en.pdf

Gall, L. (2020) 'Ending Hungary's state of emergency won't end authoritarianism bill would perpetuate rule by decree', Human Rights Watch, 29 May, https://www.hrw.org/news/2020/05/29/ending-hungarys-state-emergency-wont-end-authoritarianism

Gulyás, G. (2020) 'Minister of Prime Minister's Office, "Government seeks robust mandate with consultation"', website of the Hungarian government, 13 February, www.kormany.hu/en/prime-minister-s-office/news/government-seeks-robust-mandate-with-consultation

Hungarian Spectrum (2015) 'Hungarian Supreme Court decided: Segregation is lawful in parochial schools', 28 April, https://hungarianspectrum.org/2015/04/28/hungarian-supreme-court-decided-segregation-is-lawful-in-parochial-schools/

Hungarian Spectrum (2020a) 'A propaganda stunt: Attack on gypsies, lawyers, and prisoners', 21 January, https://hungarianspectrum.org/2020/01/21/a-propaganda-stunt-attack-on-gypsies-lawyers-and-prisoners/

Hungarian Spectrum (2020b) 'In Hungary it is Viktor Orbán who has the final word on the law', 17 January, https://hungarianspectrum.org/2020/01/17/in-hungary-it-is-viktor-orban-who-has-the-final-word-on-the-law/

Kovács, Z. (2019) 'Municipal elections – Opposition wins Budapest and makes advances in cities, Fidesz retains countryside', *Index*, 14 October, https://index.hu/english/2019/10/13/hungary_municipal_election_campaign_2019_live_coverage/

Mák, V. (2020) 'Orbán calls top court ruling in Roma segregation case "unfair"', Kafkadesk, 17 May, https://kafkadesk.org/2020/05/17/orban-calls-top-court-ruling-in-roma-segregation-case-unfair/

Miniszterelnöki Kabinetiroda (2020) 'Orbán Viktor a Kossuth Rádió „Jó reggelt, Magyarország!" című műsorában', 17 January, http://www.miniszterelnok.hu/orban-viktor-a-kossuth-radio-jo-reggelt-magyarorszag-cimu-musoraban-8/

MTI-Hungary Today (2020) 'Orbán on Gyöngyöspata case: Gov't sides with decent, working Hungarians', 31 January, https://hungarytoday.hu/orban-on-gyongyospata-case-govt-sides-with-decent-working-hungarians/

Pidd, H. (2012) 'Poor, abused and second-class: The Roma living in fear in Hungarian village', *The Guardian*, 27 January, www.theguardian.com/world/2012/jan/27/hungary-roma-living-in-fear

Radio Free Europe/Radio Liberty (2020) 'EU voices "particular concerns" over Hungary's coronavirus laws', 14 May, https://www.rferl.org/a/european-parliament-to-debate-hungary-s-coronavirus-laws-amid-detentions/30611439.html

Rorke, B. (2015) 'Separate and unequal in Hungary: "Catching up" and falling behind on Roma Inclusion', *ERRC News*, 4 September, www.errc.org/news/separate-and-unequal-in-hungary-catching-up-and-falling-behind-on-roma-inclusion

Rorke, B. (2018) 'Is Viktor Orban a racist? You decide ...', *ERRC News*, 7 March, www.errc.org/news/is-viktor-orban-a-racist-you-decide...

Rorke, B. (2020) 'Orbán steps up the hate and seeks a "robust social mandate" for antigypsyism', *ERRC*, 14 February, www.errc.org/news/orban-steps-up-the-hate-and-seeks-a-robust-social-mandate-for-antigypysism

Szurovecz, I. (2020) 'Orbán szerint igazságtalan, hogy kártérítést kaphatnak a roma gyerekek, akiket éveken át elkülönítettek az iskolában', *444.hu*, 9 January, https://444.hu/2020/01/09/orban-szerint-igazsagtalan-hogy-karteritest-kaptak-a-roma-gyerekek-akiket-eveken-at-elkulonitettek-az-iskolaban?fbclid=IwAR2C0fQtxhl_n_JiAcNY4G6jzmKO3z20xszzQdKIPIFeKsfzm7lm1bJmstY

Timmer, A. (2013) 'Horváth and Kiss v. Hungary: A strong new Roma school segregation case', *Strasbourg Observers*, 6 February, https://strasbourgobservers.com/2013/02/06/horvath-and-kiss-v-hungary-a-strong-new-roma-school-segregation-case/

Tóth, Cs. (2014) 'Some Hungarian schools to remain segregated', *The Budapest Beacon*, 25 November, https://budapestbeacon.com/hungarian-schools-remain-segregated/

UNCERD (United Nations Committee on the Elimination of Racial Discrimination) (2019) 'Concluding observations on the combined eighteenth to twenty-fifth periodic reports of Hungary', Committee on the Elimination of Racial Discrimination, Geneva, 10 May, https://tbinternet.ohchr.org/Treaties/CERD/Shared%20Documents/HUN/CERD_C_HUN_CO_18-25_34867_E.pdf

FIVE

The Romani movement: a love and vocation – Jenő Setét's reflections on a life of activism

Interviewed and translated by Katalin Rostas

Editor's introduction

Jenő Setét is one of the most prominent and experienced Romani civil rights activists in contemporary Hungary. In this edited piece, Jenő reflects on why and how he became an activist, and his hopes and aspirations for the Romani movement and people in Hungary and Europe in these challenging and troubled times.

Starting out

I have been working in this field since my youth, and it was a conscious choice after finishing high school to become an activist. So, after initially working as a decorator, I embarked upon a course for social workers at Tündérhegy, which I graduated from in 1992. Today, the programme I attended operates as a social work department at János Wesley College in Budapest. Becoming part of a social movement is like love: we do not think why it happens, it just does. My whole life is wrapped up around Romani emancipation. Why? I do not really know, but this is the aim of my life, my vocation.

Through the Romani movement, I discovered another world; for instance, in the movement, I became aware of my identity. At the summer camps of the Romani movement, I became familiar with the Romani language and culture.[1] A notable influence was Aladár Horváth. Aladár played a huge role in establishing the entire Hungarian Romani movement, defining a clear set of values centred on social justice and community action. A decade ago, my fellow campaigners and I established a non-formal movement, and in 2017, we became an association, Ide tartozunk ('We Belong Here'[2]). Its mission is to build a new type of leadership in the Romani human rights and emancipation movement. We are involved in advocacy and cultural promotion (we organize Roma Pride, a peaceful march and public demonstration around the richness of Romani culture), we provide capacity building for the community, we participate in research to investigate and understand Romani exclusion, we conduct monitoring, and we also undertake casework.

To me, Romani emancipation means ensuring equality of opportunities and social acceptance in terms of community relations and institutional practices towards Roma. So, Romani emancipation is not just an abstract sociological construct, but rather an indispensable ingredient to achieve a better life for communities. Emancipation is multifaceted and it is needed to happen in many spheres of Romani life, such as political, cultural and economic representation of the Roma.

Emancipation is measurable not only in sociological terms, but also in the presence or absence of a political, cultural and economic representation of the Roma. This is a central belief of our association.

We Belong Here association

Our association disproved many stereotypes, such as, for example, that the Roma are unable to self-organize or act without donor support. For more than a decade, we were an informal movement; we could prioritize our community ideas and interests, and value our own aims and plans. We did not care about tenders, indicators and accounting deadlines, which can often endanger creativity and stifle the community voice. However, in recent years, we became a formal organization, and this granted us the levers for change and more legitimacy for entering into negotiations with the authorities. However, all this was at the expense of flexibility and innovation in community action.

The National Democratic Institute (NDI) is where my work is based, which is a non-profit organization founded by the US State Department to promote democracy and develop civil society; the Open Society Foundation (OSF), the organization of George Soros, provided a support framework for start-up organizations and we got a small grant from them that was enough to create a tiny basic infrastructure, meaning we have an office, laptops and so on. One thing everyone needs to know: we remain guided by healthy principles and we prioritize the ideas and demands of our community centred on social justice and respect for Romani culture. If someone does not agree with our ethics, they should not fund us.

Activism and ethnicity

I think the pro-Romani organizations (non-Roma-led organizations) that help Roma are in a stronger position than Roma-led non-governmental organizations (NGOs). They have stronger economic power and ability to exert pressure, and their lobbying power is much more effective as well. The empowerment of the Roma-led NGOs is needed because, otherwise, Romani emancipation cannot be achieved, but there is no way that an equal opportunity movement can be created without a more professional, stronger representation of the community itself. It is not normal that the interests of Roma are not represented by Roma-led organizations.

On the other hand, we do have Roma-led structures that need to be reformed. I would talk about the current 'minority self-government' system, which, in our view, is incapable of representing the interests of the community as it is functioning in practice more as a 'governmental branch organization' disconnected from community realities and part of political games.

In order to change the quality of Romani self-organization, the participants need to be more honest, more resilient and better prepared, breaking with the previous political practices. Second, instead of the current paternalistic system, Romani self-organization needs to be able to attract resources without state supervision and control. Otherwise, if you pay me, I owe you a debt. If you do not pay me, but instead I raised the money, then you cannot control me. So, the Romani movement must break with the habit of expecting all resources from the state, while, at the same time, formulating its criticism of the government that runs the state. The Romani movement must create its own resources in order to have that autonomy in formulating and representing the interests of the community.

We need more social allies working alongside us. Sometimes, we Romani activists put on an ethnic robe but we also need to find common ground that connects us to non-Romani people. A social coalition and broad-based collaboration can be formed, and we need to move forward in this.

Gyöngyöspata protest

Hungary is going through difficult times as the government under Viktor Orbán has become increasingly authoritarian and Hungary is becoming a pariah among European democracies.

Orbán's system is twofold; there is a 'showcase' part, whereby its allied Romani organizations and actors benefit, namely, those in control of the local and national Romani self-government, they are his puppets![3] One of the Hungarian Roma supporting Orbán and the FIDESZ is the MEP Lívia Járóka, now Vice-President of the European Parliament. At first, we welcomed this as no Romani person has held such a high position since the existence of the European Union (EU). We were happy and wished her a lot of success. However, we have also seen with regret in recent years that party loyalty is stronger to her than her Romani identity. I find it terrible when instead of meaningful speeches or statements, she prefers party propaganda and is an apologist for what is happening in Hungary.

Since the point of Orbán's political agenda is to extract revenues from the poor and distribute it to the classes above them, the reality is that the system as a whole tends to push Romani communities downwards on an ethnic or social basis. However, it does even more damage in that they have made hatred part of the daily political routine to increase prejudice against Roma, and to create and maintain a stigmatizing and intimidating social climate against Roma as a whole, which I believe is extremely conscious political behaviour. We Belong Here organized a national protest in Budapest in February 2020 for solidarity with the Romani children of Gyöngyöspata (who have been scarred by segregation) and for the protection of an independent judiciary in Hungary. The Gyöngyöspata case relates to a Romani settlement in a rural village that attracted international attention when it suffered from far-right paramilitaries in 2011. The village has also suffered forms of segregation, leading to a court ruling that the community should receive compensation on account of school segregation. Prime Minister Viktor Orbán stated that the ruling violated the nation's 'sense of justice' and added:

[O]f course, if someone is ethnically ranked in a class, it is obviously segregation. But let's say that classifying

> someone on the basis of their capacity for education, their capacity to absorb knowledge – where there are obviously more Gypsy children in such a village – this is not segregation but catching up. (Rorke, 2020)

This was an attempt to justify segregation before the final decision of the Supreme Court had finalized its position; fortunately, despite this meddling in the legal process, the Supreme Court upheld the decision in May 2020. (For a fuller discussion of Gyöngyöspata and the state of democracy in Hungary, see Chapter Four by Rorke.)

I am old but I have never seen any movement by Roma for Roma in such huge numbers. Since the regime change in 1989, this was one of the largest civil actions made by Roma. According to media estimates, the mass protest had around 4,000–5,000 people; this is unprecedented in Hungary. We are very proud of it – that we were the ones who could achieve it – moreover, with Roma and non-Roma together.

Let us clarify what a demonstration is for. A demonstration is not a solution, but an expression of the position of a particular community's will in a given situation. We must decide whether to remain silent and thus passively assist in such an offence to human dignity and the rule of law, or we assume that we will speak out and even become a target. We Belong Here decided to take action; we wanted to express the view that a politician, neither of the Left nor of the Right, should have the right to intervene in an ongoing lawsuit. Judicial independence is such a fundamental value for us that we are determined to defend it against anyone.

The impact of the COVID-19 pandemic

We have been living in a transformed world for weeks now with the COVID-19 pandemic (time of interview, March 2020). We do not know what impact the epidemiological situation will have not only on people, but on society as a whole and on the political world. We do not know what we are up against. If the country's economy and political structure collapse, it will be similar to the post-Second World War period. I cannot estimate what impact this unprecedented situation will have; people are absorbed in their own fears and dreads, and not the question of political and social justice. Should we forget about these? No! We should not, but we need to sense that the priorities are shifting. I say this because I may have protested against the government in February but, today, I say that in this epidemiological emergency, we can do nothing but follow the government's instructions with reference to measures to save lives – however, in the long term, we must ensure our democracy is not a victim to the pandemic.[4]

I will support this government when it comes to disaster relief – be it a flood or an epidemic. However, it is also a certainty that the government cannot be disciplined by me or social movements, but the social majority can curb and shape the government and will have its chance in the 2022 election. This is something the present government should reflect upon.

The EU

There are three levels of government: local, national and international. I do not think we can ignore any of them. Given that Hungary is an EU member state, the EU has a decisive role in determining what values, what goals, it represents and how it shapes its policy.

The 2004 accession of Hungary to the EU brought with it the chance and the hope that the social exclusion, injustices and disadvantages of the Roma would be alleviated or eliminated. Sadly, the EU has proved to be weak in asserting its own democratic political and social values in the member states, and has even become a major financier of existing social inequalities by providing EU funds without human rights conditionalities and/or proper oversight of the correct use of funds, and has proven to be weak in countering state-supported racism, pogroms or hate policies. It is incredible that despite explicitly 'anti-Brussels' rhetoric, Hungary still has unhindered access to the EU's billions. It is an astonishing sin that the resources ostensibly directed at eradicating inequality are, in reality, being used to strengthen segregation and racism.

For example, in Hungary today, schools that segregate Romani children can easily and do receive EU financial support via the Hungarian government's distribution of EU funding. If the EU, even though its values uphold equality, provides financial support to schools that segregate on the basis of ethnicity, something needs to change as there seems to be a mismatch between actions and values.[5] The role of the EU cannot be left out, neither on the basis of democratic values, nor in the system of resource allocation.

Europe does not exist without nationalities, and we cannot accept a politics that does not address the Romani community. We are European, Hungarian and Roma. If you recognize only one of our three identities, we take it as a serious offence. The EU must also address the specificities of Romani communities and not cover up our existence and our problems under the authority of some kind of generalized EU 'colour-blind' social strategy because, for example, when Romani people suffer discrimination, they suffer on account of being Roma, even if they are otherwise EU citizens and if it conflicts with the EU's own directive on equal treatment. The Romani movement and the Roma have a constructive attitude towards the EU but, at the same time, we must defend our own interests very strongly vis-à-vis the EU and a New Social Europe.

Editor's conclusion

The interview with Jenő Setét demonstrates the passion and dynamism at the Romani grass roots but also support for the concepts and principles promoted in this book, namely, the need for the empowerment and self-organization of marginalized citizens and solidarity in these challenging and turbulent times.

Notes

[1] The modern Romani movement in Hungary was started in 1957 by Mária László, who sought to fight against racial discrimination and for equal rights through cultural means. Between 1978 and 2008, János Bársony and Ágnes Daróczi, respected activists working for Romani rights, as well as several others, organized cultural camps for the Romani community, which aimed to strengthen Romani identity.

[2] See: https://idetartozunk.org/we-belong-here-association/

[3] In Hungary, there is a system of local Romani minority self-governments and a national one that was established in 1993 and funded by the state. These give largely advisory platforms to the Roma. It is dominated by a pro-Orbán faction called Lungo Drom. Critics have complained about state interference and a lack of capacity building and internal democracy (Kovats, 2000).

[4] The Orbán administration assumed unprecedented powers in the midst of the COVID-19 crisis, allowing the current FIDESZ government to rule by decree and the possibility of being imprisoned for up to five years for spreading disinformation, a measure tantamount to an attack on free speech and independent journalism.

[5] The Central European Roma Civil Monitor reported in its 2020 synthesis report that EU funding has been given to schools that uphold segregation in Hungary.

References

Kovats, M. (2000) 'The political significance of the first national Gypsy minority self-government in Hungary', *Contemporary Politics*, 6(3): 247–62.

Rorke, B. (2020) 'Orbán weighs in against court ruling and calls for justice for segregationists', European Roma Rights Centre, 10 January, www.errc.org/news/orban-weighs-in-against-court-ruling-and-calls-for-justice-for-segregationists

SIX

Romani young people's activism and transformative change

Anna Daróczi, Lisa Smith and Sarah Cemlyn

Introduction

This chapter arose from conversations between two Romani women activists working with young people (Daróczi and Smith) and a non-Romani woman researcher (Cemlyn). It considers lessons for transformative change from empowerment work with young Roma. Daróczi and Smith led the direction through their knowledge, ideas and direct experience, and Cemlyn framed the content. Broader personal reflections are indicated through direct quotations from Daróczi and Smith.

We outline four underpinning approaches: terminological issues relating to the groups we focus on; discrimination and inequality affecting Romani young people; the conceptual framework informing the discussion; and the current policy framework for empowerment work by and with Romani youth. We describe selected areas of work in national and international contexts through the organizations with which Daróczi and Smith are involved. We then analyse and reflect on these currents and contexts of activism under themes of: empowerment; identity and diversity in Romani movements; Roma/non-Roma solidarity; and policy implications. The conclusion focuses on new and inspirational directions for Romani young people's activism.

Note on terminology

We take a cross-national perspective through the work of a European organization, Phiren Amenca, working in ten countries, and a group of UK organizations, including *Travellers' Times* (TT) youth section and Roma Rights Defenders. The umbrella term 'Roma' has increasingly been used by the European Commission and other institutions to include groups in both Eastern and Western Europe. Simhandl (2006) refers to inherent silences and unspoken assumptions about boundaries around essentialist categories concerning these groups in European Union (EU) political discourse. There are numerous groups from Western Europe to the Balkans who do not identify as 'Roma'; however, as an endonym, it has been widely adopted (see Chapter One).

'Roma' is used inside Phiren Amenca, and often across Europe in relation to pan-European policy development and civil society networking. Within the UK, however, it has been common to refer to 'Gypsies, Roma and Travellers' (GRT), of which Gypsies and Travellers have a tradition of commercial nomadism, whereas 'Roma' signifies largely sedentary groups entering the UK from Eastern and Central Europe over three decades but with strong connections to some UK Romani Gypsy groups. An alternative umbrella term adopted by the Council of Europe (CoE) Commissioner for Human Rights (2012) is 'Roma and Travellers', which includes the wide variety of groups its work covers. The dynamic between self-definition/representation and externally applied terms and boundaries is inherent to the political process of self-empowerment and activism (McGarry, 2014). With reference to terminology, we refer to racism directed at Roma/Gypsies and Travellers as 'antigypsyism' (for wider discussion, see Chapter Three by Taba) but retain 'anti-Gypsyism' in quotes.

Inequality and discrimination

Inequality and antigypsyism have intensified in recent decades despite policy measures such as the National Roma Integration Strategies (NRIS). The Fundamental Rights Agency (FRA) has reported stark statistics on the exclusion experienced by Roma (see Chapter One).

The European Youth Forum (2014) explored young people's experiences of discrimination across multiple domains and dimensions, including gender, ethnicity, lesbian, gay, bisexual and trans (LGBT), and refugee status. Being 18–24 years old was itself considered grounds for discrimination, magnified by intersectional experiences. A total of 55.7 per cent saw Roma as discriminated against generally, as the most discriminated group in terms of education, qualifications and renting accommodation, and as highly discriminated against in health and other services. The multifaceted denial of rights, opportunities and affirmation means that Romani young people are 'denied the right to be young' (Phiren Amenca, 2016: 6) because they lack space to explore freely and develop their own identities, characters and aspirations.

The FRA's (2013) analysis of 2008 and 2012 surveys reveals the compounding of discrimination by gender, reporting lower levels of literacy (77 per cent, compared to 85 per cent), post-16 education (37 per cent, as against 50 per cent) and employment (21 per cent, compared to 85 per cent) for Romani women than for men. Jovanović et al (2015: 3), discussing the diversity and complexity of the Romani Women's Movement, relate how intersectionality theory has helped make sense of the 'hybrid structures of inequalities Romani women face', identified lacunae and challenged the general (white/non-Romani) discourse of the feminist movement, the general (often patriarchal) discourse of the Romani movement and the broader patriarchy. Jovanović and Daróczi (2015) highlight how much more work is needed to develop the strengths of a truly intersectional Romani movement. Jovanović et al (2015) also refer to tensions between older and younger Roma, possibly related to the latter moving away from conservative and restrictive discourses concerning women's roles. LGBT Roma/Gypsies have explored how these identities can lead to exclusion or invisibility within both Romani and LGBT communities, and the struggle to assert and celebrate these identities (Baker, 2015).

Educational opportunities to open doors to future active citizenship are systematically denied to Roma in many European countries (Cemlyn and Ryder, 2016). Segregation in separate classes/schools and misclassification as pupils with special educational needs remain key obstacles in many countries (see Chapter One). Infringement proceedings were launched by the European Commission against the Czech Republic, Slovakia and Hungary in 2014, 2015 and 2016, respectively; however, so far they have resulted in cosmetic rather than meaningful change (ERRC, 2017).

In England, ineffective mainstreaming policy approaches, coupled with austerity – as seen in the demise of nationwide local authority Traveller education support services by 2018 – have left youth with no targeted education support or information, and a loss of knowledge on identity and inclusion within educational institutions. The UK 'Race disparity audit' (Gov.UK, 2017) highlighted stark inequality of educational and health outcomes. In 2018, the United Nations Special Rapporteur on Racism noted that Gypsies and Travellers had the highest rates of fixed and permanent exclusions, alongside informal exclusions, arising from negative teacher stereotypes, low teacher expectations and the absence of ethnic and cultural representations in the curriculum (United Nations, 2018). In the first national survey of prejudice in Britain for over ten years, the Equality and Human Rights Commission (2018) showed that more people openly expressed negative feelings towards GRT (44 per cent) than any other group of people in society. Rising antigypsyism continues to be fuelled by media depictions of Gypsies and Travellers as threatening 'invaders' of local communities, and has manifested in local and national politics, with recent government proposals to criminalize a nomadic existence further (Gov.UK, 2020).

Conceptual framework

This chapter is based on the key concepts of human rights, interculturalism, empowerment and antigypsyism. The international and European human rights framework, incorporating civil-political, socio-economic and representational rights (Cemlyn, 2008), underpins Romani youth campaigns, like other movements for social justice (Donnelly, 2007). There is a dynamic between top-down convention-framed human rights work and grass-roots, bottom-up struggles (Ife and Fiske, 2006).

While human rights can be flouted by regressive regimes and right-wing movements, and perceived divisively by majority groups in relation to minority groups (Bell and Cemlyn, 2014), there are also left-wing critiques. These include: their assumed universality; postcolonial arguments concerning imperialist imposition on non-Western countries (Gosavi, 2016); and anti-capitalist arguments of its co-option by neoliberalism, consumerization and privatization, with human rights, free markets and democracy being a widely accepted triad, despite exacerbation of poverty and human rights violations (Evans and Ayers, 2006). The EU has focused on economic inclusion of Roma within neoliberalism but continuing social and political marginalization undermines this aim from within.

Therefore 'the notion of human rights ... [is] subject to both historical and social contexts' (Gosavi, 2016: 63) and there are 'many defensible implementations' (Donnelly, 2007: 299). The notion of 'human security' (Yuval-Davis, 2014), drawing on development and capabilities studies (Sen, 1999), also incorporates emotional dimensions, the need for belonging and safety from violence, alongside recognition and redistribution. The Romani rights movement and Romani feminist, LGBTIQ and youth movements negotiate these complexities but the human rights framework remains a strong foundation for all campaigns.

Postcolonial theory links to interculturalism, a core approach for activist projects, alongside intersectionality. While 'multiculturalism' mainly celebrates difference and can essentialize and exclude (Cantle, 2012), interculturalism refers to constant and equal dialogue between different groups mutually influencing and modifying each other, and seeks to transform unequal power relationships between minority and majority groups, and enable mutual adaptation rather than one-way integration into a flawed dominant system. Although even multiculturalism is currently seen as dangerous to national identity in state policies and programmes in Hungary, a few small civil society projects do adopt an intercultural approach, mostly educational and sensitizing events where organizers bring together Roma and non-Roma for building dialogue and cooperation between them, while utilizing the experiences and knowledge of the Romani participants/facilitators as expert input.

Intersectionality developed from critical race feminism and postcolonial theory as a challenge to essentialist identity politics in the Black movement (Anthias and Yuval-Davis, 1983), and is a tool in understanding multiple identities and generating a 'transversal politics' that facilitates reflexive dialogue between people of different positionalities (Yuval-Davis, 1999). However, there remains a role, albeit contested, for strategic essentialism in the struggle of marginalized identities for social justice (Brubaker, 2004). In the state socialist era, cultural preservation was the only flag under which Roma could officially gather in Hungary; today, for many national and international organizations, a cultural focus also still seems to be the only politically viable way to advocate for Roma's own institutions.

Dynamic change also informs notions of empowerment. It can focus on individual development of skills, awareness and confidence in taking control of one's own life (for example, Zimmerman, 1990) but also be co-opted by state systems as a regulatory or oppressive rather than emancipatory tool (Baistow, 1994). Here, we focus on collective empowerment and analysis encompassing individual self-empowerment, reflecting also Freire's (1972) critical pedagogy and development of critical consciousness. Empowerment of Roma has become part of European policymaking goals but reality has not matched rhetoric in incorporating Romani voices in policies and programmes (Acton et al, 2014).

There are related critiques of how Romani civil society has become distorted by 'NGO-ization', dominated by donor agendas, remote from the Romani grass roots and preoccupied by specific interventions (Trehan, 2009). Those organizations that are closer to their constituencies have struggled, reduced services or closed because of austerity cuts 'at a time when demand for these services is increasing considerably' (EWL, 2012: 14).

The barriers faced by Roma are magnified in the broader context of antigypsyism. End (2012) explores its role historically and currently as a majority society mechanism to stabilize itself through projecting uncertainty onto a minority population, framing a notion of Roma – unconnected to reality – as having unstable identities and lifestyles or a 'non-identity', being 'parasitic' in the sense of non-productive, and having an absence of discipline.

Youth empowerment policy

The definition of youth empowerment of the United Nations Children's Fund (UNICEF, 2018) refers to young people's leadership, mutual connectivity and support. The CoE (2015a: 13) more clearly asserts a human rights framework, claiming a pioneering role in mainstreaming human rights education in youth policy and practice generally, and that this 'provides the optimal educational approach and content to understanding human rights as a common asset of all humanity and, conversely, to understanding the violations of the human rights of anyone as a violation of the human rights of all'.

Human rights education and combating antigypsyism are at the core of the CoE's (2011) *Roma Youth Action Plan*, developed from recognition that Romani youth had no specific support channels, either in mainstream youth councils or within Romani forums (Phiren Amenca, 2016). Thus, the goal has been 'double mainstreaming ... [to] ensure, on the one hand, the inclusion of youth issues in Roma policies and programmes and, on the other, that of Roma youth issues into youth policies' (CoE, 2011: 2). The plan is elaborated around six themes, 'strengthening Roma youth identity; addressing multiple discrimination and recognising multiple identities; building a stronger Roma youth movement; increasing the capacity of Roma youth organisations to participate in policy making; human rights and human rights education; combating discrimination and antigypsyism' (CoE, 2015b: 10). It references the need to help young people identify and challenge structural discrimination, combat racist attitudes, build self-esteem, and increase human rights awareness and support to remove obstacles (CoE, 2015a), but it is an uphill task.

One of the principles outlined in guidelines for the *Roma Youth Action Plan* (2016–20) is 'Participation and consultation of Roma youth and Roma youth organisations, from the local to the European level, including their involvement in policy advocacy' (CoE, 2016: 4). However, until 2019, the Hungarian Youth Council had no Romani lead member. Similarly, the first Romani member of the European Youth Forum joined in January 2020. Meanwhile, the EU Youth Guarantee is economically focused, namely, that all young people under 25 receive a good-quality offer of employment, continued education, apprenticeship or traineeship within four months of becoming unemployed or leaving formal education (European

Commission, 2018), but there is only limited evidence of these objectives being fulfilled for Roma.

Case studies: youth empowerment work internationally and within the UK

The main mission of Phiren Amenca is to build dialogue and engagement between Romani and non-Romani youth and organizations as a tool for youth participation in public and political life, to advocate for double mainstreaming, and to challenge stereotypes, racism and antigypsyism. Funded by the European Commission and the CoE, it is an international network of Romani and non-Romani volunteers and voluntary service organizations, with members in ten countries (within and outside the EU) and partner organizations beyond. 'Phiren Amenca' is a Romani expression meaning 'come and share a journey with us'. This journey is personal, its space and length are different, but the final aim is the respect that develops between Roma and non-Roma.

Phiren Amenca's work rests on three pillars: voluntary service, non-formal education methods and advocacy. Voluntary service coordinates nine to 12 months of exchange of Romani and non-Romani volunteers between Romani and mainstream non-governmental organizations (NGOs). The educational programme involves seminars, training and conferences for volunteers, activists, youth workers, educators, and professionals about: racism and antigypsyism; human rights; intersectionality; challenging stereotypes; and Romani history – Remembrance and the Roma Genocide. In advocacy, Phiren Amenca trains, supports and empowers young people, and builds the advocacy capacities of organizations on local, regional and European levels. Connections are built with decision-making bodies, advocacy groups and organizations, though Phiren Amenca lacks capacity for steady, strategic work in this field. Together with the youth, it conducts research and drafts policy recommendations for intergovernmental bodies (for example, CoE and EU) and for national decision-making structures through its member organizations. As Daróczi notes:

'Our vision is totally in line with the concept of a Social Europe. Our work with Roma youth is self-empowerment at its best: through our seminars, local activities and international events, we give them tools and knowledge they can use in order to participate, represent their own interests, advocate for their needs and their rights. Given the diversity of needs and interest among Roma youth, the main issue is the lack of access to decision-making processes where Roma youth could vocalize their needs, whatever they may be. Through voluntary service, Roma young people can get to know and practise how NGOs work, what the structures of local or EU policymaking are, and how local communities can be organized around social justice causes. Personal contact is essential, to trust and support young people in moving on with their own ideas.... This ... entails sharing and transferring power as we would like the young people to take our place. There is a need to be more courageous, enable young people's contributions, listen to young people when shaping our methods, facilitate young Roma being in the lead.... We also promote an attitude with non-Roma volunteers and seminar participants which does not position them as "the saviours" of Roma, but as partners, where Roma are the ones knowing what they need and the agents of their actions. White folks are not there to teach or help them, but to assist and accompany them on the way.'

Daróczi also reflects on the constraints of a neoliberal and antigypsyist economic context, EU policy structures, and limited staff resources:

'The EU volunteer programme's main goal is to provide skills and knowledge to the youngsters which they can later use in the job market, and as a side goal, they also acquire intercultural skills, learn to be tolerant, etc. It would be nice if tolerance were a job-market skill too. Our projects have to prepare youth for the job market but ... many of them will have no chance to get a job because of hate and antigypsyism ... we prepare them for a labour market which is not prepared for them ... when the young people go back home, they can rarely stay optimistic as their realities do not provide them with high hopes.'

Equally:

'We organize international seminars ... to give them advocacy tools and opportunities to participate in decision-making processes, for which one needs a mindset of goals, dreams, visions and practical skills. We try to increase their involvement ... but we are very limited because the space for citizenship participation is shrinking, let alone for Roma youth.... With the authoritarianization of states, the number of democratic tools and the number of people brave enough to use them are decreasing.... It is still not evident to invite Roma youth advocates or organizations to forums where Roma and/or youth policies are discussed and decisions made. When invited ... we do not always have the resources to participate meaningfully [or] keep the young people we prepared in the loop.'

TT (*Travellers' Times*, 2018a) is a national media and communications project. TT produces a biannual print magazine and daily website. It is a long-standing project of Rural Media, a charitable production company creating issue-driven films and heritage and digital arts projects that support people to acquire practical digital skills, participate in cultural production and influence change. Funded by the Big Lottery, it was set up to challenge negative representations of GRT in mainstream media and is designed, predominantly written by and features GRT communities, giving a platform to promote positive imagery, challenge stereotypes and provide support, tools and opportunity for self-advocacy.

A consultation with beneficiaries identified a demand by older Roma and Travellers that young people were the 'future generation' and resources should be put into supporting them to get their voices heard. In response, Youth at Travellers' Times (YTT) was also developed as a website platform for youth journalism and media production for young people to develop media skills, news-writing courses and events to train young people to tell their stories. A national youth advisory group was established to ensure the youth section was led by beneficiaries. This attracted a pool of young, proactive Roma and Traveller activists, from varying backgrounds, with some from activist families and others finding out later about the network of organizations supporting GRT communities. A small network of activists emerged and TT created a space for peer-to-peer support and mentoring to develop, alongside training in youth journalism and digital safety, and for self-advocacy and access to information about European training and study sessions. However, the project's media focus sets limits on how TT can support their activism and there is disconnection from the European opportunities that TT promotes. As Smith comments:

'Often, funding priorities can act as a barrier to supporting young activists' ambitions, so we work hard to find creative ways to establish new spin-off projects that are community-driven and youth-led. To my knowledge, there is no youth organization specifically targeted at Roma and Travellers in the UK that equips youth with tools in strategic advocacy, promotion of political engagement and its relevance to their lived context, challenging and recognizing antigypsyism, building knowledge on how the NGO sector operates for youth to develop their own project ideas and access funding mechanisms. I see this type of work being essential to the development of the Romani movement in the UK; otherwise, we have young activists being pulled into all different sorts of projects but with no guidance on a coordinated approach to their advocacy, or focus on how their own personal aspirations and ambitions can be supported and harnessed.

Youth rarely take the opportunity [of training sessions in Europe], though we have had a few individual cases where young people have gone to study sessions in Budapest through promotion of events via TT and it has been "life-changing". My perception is that there is minimal knowledge about the existence of the Council of Europe and the *Roma Youth Action Plan* and the benefits it can present amongst youth in the UK. I question if the terminology of "Roma" when advertising prevents participation of young people who identify as "Gypsy" or "Traveller".… Either they don't understand how it can relate to their lived context or the promotion of events is simply not reaching them. My concern is that Brexit will result in further isolation and reduced capacity for Roma and Traveller youth to develop European networks of solidarity and support.'

The 2019 It's Kushti to Rokker project was designed to raise awareness about how high levels of social and educational exclusion and antigypsyism impact young people's mental health and wellbeing. After consulting with young people in 2018, the YTT Advisory Group recognized that there was a clear lack of video-based informative content that accurately reflected young Gypsies' and Travellers' own perspectives on their lived experiences. In the project, young people worked with writers and filmmakers to create a series of five short films based on their experiences, addressing education, bereavement, online hate and double layers of discrimination. The impact of racial discrimination on well-being, feelings of self-perception and self-worth was an overarching theme.

An accompanying information pack provided advice and signposting to support for young people and families. Furthermore, a ten-minute documentary for policymakers and education and health professionals aimed to raise awareness of the inequalities and antigypsyism Romani and Traveller youth experience, and the impact on mental health risks. Also, a downloadable toolkit supported the facilitation of discussions on mental well-being, and offered resources promoting Romani and Traveller history, language and culture.

Romani and Traveller youth involved in the project were supported to lead a series of screenings across the UK attended by policymakers and health and education providers. The youth-led production process enabled the viewer to see the subject through young people's eyes, facilitated discussions about mental health, combatted feelings of isolation and offered a creative approach to addressing challenging issues.

The YTT Advisory Group also engaged in wider European organizing. An activist from the European Roma Rights Centre (ERRC) was invited by Smith to talk with the other young activists about his experiences working in Central and Eastern Europe and the situation for Roma. They joined forces in July 2018 at Appleby Horse Fair to support the ERRC in launching Roma Rights Defenders (2018) in the UK, a pan-European activist network of Roma and non-Roma (*Travellers' Times*, 2018b), through which 'we can share and receive information, collaborate, and mobilise strategically against Roma rights violations'. Smith commented that "To my knowledge, this is the first international network of this kind established in the UK."

A small group of Romani activist Labour Party members formed alliances through political advocacy and engagement with parliamentary allies. The 2017 Labour manifesto stated that 'We will end racism and discrimination against Gypsy, Roma and Traveller communities, and protect the right to lead a nomadic way of life' (Labour Party, 2017: 112), and many were prompted to vote for the first time. Progress was slow but a Labour 'friends of' group developed to provide official representation and knowledge, and crucially to create spaces for community activism within the party. As Smith comments: "This type of independent advocacy is important for the Romani movement as a whole ... the term 'antigypsyism' has not been recognized or adopted by the UK government and is a fundamental step towards acknowledging the situation of its Gypsy, Roma and Traveller populations."

Discussion

Human rights and Roma empowerment in a European context

The account of Phiren Amenca's work illustrates implementation of several principles of the CoE's (2011) *Roma Youth Action Plan*: addressing and combatting multiple discrimination and antigypsyism; human rights education; strengthening Romani youth identity; building a stronger Romani youth movement; and increasing the capacity of Romani youth organizations to participate in policymaking. Together with opportunities offered for intercultural dialogue, educational engagement in civil society organizations and support to develop their own initiatives, this kind of inspiring empowerment work, if multiplied and well resourced across Europe, could make a noticeable difference to the resources, strengths and skills of Romani youth, and consequently their ability to promote transformative change. Moreover, the advocacy and networking opportunities offered by larger, donor-funded NGOs such as the ERRC (albeit that NGOs are sometimes found to distort grass-roots momentum), as well as educational seminars for

Roma like those at the Central European University (CEU), enhance the apparent benefits of European connectedness and cooperation, and can be 'life-changing' for individuals.

For Smith, in the UK, "We are lacking training in policy advocacy that guides Romani and Traveller activists in a structured approach to tackling systemic issues surrounding education and health that would enhance their grass-roots activism." Therefore, the European examples of processes and structures represent a possible new model:

> 'for improving the life chances of Roma and Traveller communities across Europe. Shall we also start investing in more advanced forms of youth empowerment and mobilization and learn from organizations like ERGO, Ternype (which provides in-depth reflections on antigypsyism through a Roma Genocide education lens) and Phiren Amenca in their approaches and relationships?'

However, Daróczi's experience also illustrates the current limits of this model because of constraints on Phiren Amenca and similar organizations, through insufficient resources and staffing, to follow through on higher-level opportunities for young people to influence policy, lack of support for them after involvement in the project, and the antigypsyist context limiting access to jobs, with reality not providing "high hopes". Moreover, there are wider dangers in the rise of right-wing politics and increasing racism. At the same time, smaller and independent activist initiatives, as in the UK, suggest sources of energy and determination to enable the Romani voice regardless of lack of support.

Barriers, tensions and challenges to empowerment within civil society

These discussions evidenced a number of challenges for civil society and the work of NGOs, including funding and firefighting pressures, organizational objectives, and internal tensions, together with pointers towards more powerful activism. Civil society can be conceptualized as radical and transformative, but in the context of austerity and antigypsyism, it may primarily be dealing with immediate issues of health, employment, accommodation and violence, without opportunities for strategic work and with declining funding. Activists can sometimes shape organizational opportunities to promote change, though within limits. TT is a media rather than a human rights organization, so despite the youth group stretching its brief, it is unsuited to sustaining direct activism.

However, even with relatively secure, albeit circumscribed, funding and empowerment objectives, as at Phiren Amenca, conflicts can arise with workers' own activist values. Despite the overall balance of positives that many on the Left (not all) would ascribe to EU membership, it remains a neoliberal, capitalist project. For workers like Daróczi who envision a more equitable non-capitalist system, this can create a contradiction: "Personally, sometimes it is hard to operate from EU funds while being anti-capitalist. The EU is first and foremost a [capitalist] economic union, and we keep trying to decorate this base with some values of human rights and tolerance and justice." Alternative fundraising approaches raise similar dilemmas: "One could go for other ways of raising funds but we cannot afford a professional fundraiser; plus, I don't know how I feel about approaching companies, such as Coca Cola or the like." The project-based system undermines fundamental change:

'Civil society organizations should play a key role in transformative change but the project-based operation makes it almost impossible. You either have to set aside your strategic goals or not comply with the grant's objectives. So, you either define your goals, as an organization, in line with those of the donors, or your work is considered not needed.'

The UK experienced a rapid withdrawal of the state from service provision, especially in the years 2010 to 2020, through increased privatization and drastic budget cuts to local authorities and other bodies. Civil society has a crucial role in picking up on deficits in government services but NGOs do not have the capacity or resources for such a role, which would also further divert them into firefighting and away from wider change. Moreover, there are systemic barriers for Romani young people's involvement in these organizations. A no-deal Brexit might result in even deeper cuts.

Autonomous Roma-led groups across Europe are supporting communities and exposing antigypsyism and historical wrongs. In the UK, a small but growing population of educated and politically engaged young Roma and Travellers are challenging the status quo and want to take an active role in building up their communities. They are bypassing NGOs and creating their own advocacy structures and relationships with politicians, supported by non-GRT allies, but can meet some resistance from the NGO sector. Projects built and sustained by well-meaning *gadje* can be less than empowering and sometimes instead promote a culture of dependence. Young activists face a gap of organizations offering tools of agency and self-advocacy that place knowledge into the hands of the individuals themselves. As Audre Lorde (1984: 110) said, 'the master's tools will never dismantle the master's house'. For Smith:

'It feels like we are at a significant time in the movement … many NGOs are being challenged on how they are supporting the development of Romani and Traveller youth to eventually move into positions of leadership and employ more community members. In order to allow the Romani and Traveller movement in the UK to develop further we must acknowledge some parts of the sector are outdated, and space and support must be given for new community-led initiatives and ideas to thrive, with young leaders at the forefront who nurture and strengthen Roma and Traveller youth activism and identity, building on and developing links with the Council of Europe, *Roma Youth Action Plan* and European Roma youth organizations.'

Therefore, while NGOs can relieve hardship, help people to negotiate within the parameters set by the system and stretch those limits a little, they may fail to transcend barriers to empowerment such as inaccessible labour markets, be more individually based than collectively transformative, or fail to adapt and empower Romani leadership. They fit into a broader oppressive system in contradictory ways, helping to sustain it by alleviating some pressure (Daróczi et al, 2018). Yet, civil society more broadly is crucial both to protecting basic rights and to radical democratic and transformative change, with grass-roots autonomous initiatives breaking through boundaries.

Romani movements, identity, diversity, intersectionality and intercultural solidarity

The experience of different organizations illustrates fruitful cross-currents, as well as challenges in relation to identity, diversity, intersectional and intercultural exchange, and the development of Romani movements. Phiren Amenca celebrates culture but focuses away from identity politics to common human rights across differences. This is partly practical since young people sometimes come from more than ten countries with different traditions, values and identity constructions, but also because their mission is empowerment, activism and dialogue-building. Their educational events demonstrate that Roma have culturally and geographically diverse identities but should cooperate and fight together for recognition. Politically, identity politics and movements have also taken various directions, with Romani (youth) activism more focused on nation-building in some countries and on universal human rights in others. This causes tensions and the organization's goal is the opposite: to create dialogue and community – for that, the common denominator is human rights, even though universalist values might discourage certain types of activism.

In its external relationships, Phiren Amenca builds alliances with other groups, ethnic, national and religious minorities, LGBTIQ communities, feminist organizations, and so on. This can be difficult, especially if they focus on specific identities rather than common themes, because other groups are not necessarily favourable to Roma, so the common aims of human rights – the right to recognition and redistribution – are more helpful when creating cooperative spaces and alliances, though the continuing emphasis on multiculturalism and identity politics in the global arena of minority groups makes this harder. At the organizational level too, despite a highly diverse membership of the international network, differences become an asset, and the human rights culture mediates any conflicts.

Similarly, at YTT, self-representation promotes non-homogeneous views of diverse ethnic groups and is a means to highlight diversity and intersectionality. Roma Rights Defenders and other groups include diverse ethnicities, as encompassed in the term 'Gypsies, Roma, Travellers'.

However, there is a persistent threat to a nomadic existence, including: the UK government's tighter creation of 'gypsy status' for planning purposes, which many saw as a direct attempt to 'define Gypsy and Traveller communities out of existence' (*Travellers' Times*, 2016); measures restricting travelling and Traveller self-employment; and, more recently, current proposals to criminalize trespass (Gov.UK, 2020). Therefore, identity can be used as a mechanism for cultural perseverance related to nomadic heritage, which becomes a shield for some against a society that views them as 'out of date'.

Although 'Romani movement' is not a frequent term in the UK, and might suggest NGOs often not led by community members, there have been advances since the 1990s. Across the UK and Europe, technology and social media have furnished opportunities to gather and tell varied, intersectional experiences and provide collective support, increasing awareness and networking. When it can move away from front-line work and public awareness campaigns, this movement may develop a more complex approach, providing opportunities for Romani and Traveller youth to reflect on issues around human rights and equip them with tools for collective mobilization and the self-empowerment that comes through being part of a collective battle.

GRT civil society has played a critical role in nurturing and developing a prominent feature of the growing Romani and Traveller movement, namely, the predominant number of GRT women working and volunteering within civil society, including at TT. These activists vary on how they self-define as feminist but are increasingly coming together across different groups. However, Smith notes how "funding constraints and the need just to get the job done mean many voices are silenced, or dominated within the sector by non-GRT allies who are not conscious of power imbalances and dominate meetings, unintentionally disempowering GRT women by speaking on their behalf".

Some advances in raising awareness of LGBTIQ experiences in the UK include Gypsy-authored research among Gypsy gay men (Baker, 2015). More recently, Traveller Pride was founded in 2019 as a self-organized network collective of Roma and Travellers to provide a platform for community intersectionality and 'advice, guidance, support and information to make life easier for LGBT+ Travellers' (Traveller Pride, 2019). On 6 July 2019, Traveller Pride marched at Pride London, the first official representation of Travellers in the UK at a Pride march. The 2019 Its Kushti to Rokker project captured the historic occasion through a short film, 'Hard Road to Travel', based on the lived experiences of those involved and aimed at promoting visibility of intersectional identities.

In Hungary and elsewhere in Europe, many successful Romani NGOs are led by women but it is an underpaid sector. In Daróczi's experience, male leaders are more numerous where NGOs have more secure funding and higher pay. In parts of Europe, there is a clearer identification of Romani feminism than currently in the UK, and this balance is reflected in the staff composition of Phiren Amenca. Four women manage the network who either identify as or effectively operate as feminists. Being led by women has a high impact on their work as they always keep in mind, and talk/train about gender equality, feminisms in their various forms and intersectionality. This includes conscious decisions about supporting Romani girls' and women's participation, for example, including a male relative in activities in cases where traditional families will not allow a girl to travel alone, and making efforts to secure the representation of LGBTIQ Romani individuals or groups at events, which might not happen with Hungarian male staff.

Yuval-Davis (2014) has argued that part of the oppression of women is that they are constructed 'as embodiments of collectivity boundaries' but that this 'might make it easier for women to transcend and cross boundaries and engage in dialogical transversal politics'. This dynamic – the opportunity to experiment, challenge and form new connections across boundaries that comes with marginalized status – is often evident in the Romani women's and youth movements, though less so as yet in the developing LGBTIQ movement.

Alongside the complexity of exchanges across different Romani ethnicities and intersectional positionalities lies the question of solidarity with non-Romani allies, which can be problematic where non-Roma are unaware of dominating, but alternatively supportive and respectful of Romani leadership, as in the independent advocacy examples, the structured approach of Phiren Amenca and elsewhere (Daróczi et al, 2018). This returns to questions of transformative change. The examples of powerful Romani activism point to more fundamental challenges to systemic oppression that reverse rather than mitigate it. In Daróczi's words:

'It is time for white people, men, straight folks to integrate to the society which is non-white, non-male, etc in majority. As long as we think of ourselves who need to be integrated to messed-up societies and systems, we cannot talk about empowerment. If we want transformative change, we cannot seek the one-sided integration of the oppressed into a system which was built to create and maintain inequalities.'

Policy implications

In most countries, the policy environment is not favourable to the needs and interests of Romani youth. Phiren Amenca has been advocating with others for the representation of Romani youth in policymaking and decision-making structures. National youth councils, the European Youth Forum and all mainstream youth organizations should reflect on how their structures contribute to strengthening Romani youth participation, as well as the internal barriers. Advocacy work by Romani youth organizations locally, nationally and internationally requires recognition.

Since the European Commission launched the EU Framework for NRIS in 2011, institutional racism has continued to manifest itself through policies and practices. The NRIS after 2020 should have a clear focus on Romani youth, participation structures, non-formal education, mobility and support for Romani youth organizations. The NRIS in some countries, for example, Slovenia and Croatia, started to develop this focus. Organizations such as Phiren Amenca and TernYpe indicate tested methods for developing critical awareness, participation, dialogue and activism.

Intersectional identities and issues for young Roma need to have dedicated space in policy discussions. While attention to gender has proved crucial in mobilization, LGBTIQ Roma face violence and ostracism by families/Romani community members, discrimination from majority society, as well as exclusion from mainstream LGBTIQ organizations (Tišer, 2015).

Conclusion

A step change is needed to support young people's involvement in transformative change based on the premise of 'nothing about us without us'. A wider concept of Social Europe that moves away from the shackles of neoliberalism to foreground equality, dialogue, redistribution and respectful recognition of all minority perspectives is needed to underpin greater progress.

The energy and dynamism for such change is ready in a range of social movement and civil society initiatives highlighting the potential of Romani young people and movements to be in the vanguard. There are continuing dangers from antigypsyism, and increased threats from racist populist and nationalist political movements, while a hard Brexit may lead to more regressive and unregulated UK policy and add further challenges to solidarity networks for transformative change. It is vital to keep these channels and networks flourishing that enable Romani young people to learn from and with each other, resist the disempowering messages of their social and political environment, and hope and act for change that will break out of the current system. While young activists need support to maximize their activism, the changes they create must be in their hands.

References

Acton, T., Rostas, I. and Ryder, A. (2014) 'The Roma in Europe: The debate over the possibilities for empowerment to seek social justice', in A. Ryder, S. Cemlyn and T. Acton (eds) *Hearing the Voices of Gypsy, Roma and Traveller Communities*, Bristol: Policy Press, pp 177–96.

Anthias, F. and Yuval-Davis, N. (1983) 'Contextualising feminism: Gender, ethnic & class divisions', *Feminist Review*, 15: 62–75.

Baistow, K. (1994) 'Liberation and regulation? Some paradoxes of empowerment', *Critical Social Policy*, 42: 34–46.

Baker, D. (2015) 'The queer Gypsy', in M. Bogdán, J. Dunajeva, T. Junghaus, A. Kóczé, M. Rövid, I. Rostas, A. Ryder and M.T. Szilvási (eds) *Nothing About Us without Us: Roma Participation in Policy Making and Knowledge Production*, Budapest: European Roma Rights Centre, http://www.errc.org/roma-rights-journal/roma-rights-2-2015-nothing-about-us-without-us-roma-participation-in-policy-making-and-knowledge-production

Bell, K. and Cemlyn, S. (2014) 'Developing public support for human rights in the United Kingdom: Reasserting the importance of socioeconomic rights', *International Journal of Human Rights*, 18(7/8): 822–41.

Brubaker, R. (2004) *Ethnicity without Groups*, Cambridge, MA: Harvard University Press.

Cantle, T. (2012) *Interculturalism: The New Era of Cohesion and Diversity*, Basingstoke: Palgrave Macmillan.

Cemlyn, S. (2008) 'Human rights practice: Possibilities and pitfalls for developing emancipatory social work', *Ethics and Social Welfare*, 2(3): 222–42.

Cemlyn, S. and Ryder, A. (2016) 'Education for citizenship and social justice: The case of Gypsies, Travellers and Roma', in A. Peterson, R. Hattam, M. Zembylas and J. Arthur (eds) *The Palgrave International Handbook of Education for Citizenship and Social Justice*, London: Palgrave Macmillan, pp 163–85.

CoE (Council of Europe) (2011) *Roma Youth Action Plan*, Strasbourg: CoE.

CoE (2012) *Human Rights of Roma and Travellers in Europe*, Strasbourg: CoE, https://rm.coe.int/the-human-rights-of-roma-and-travellers-in-europe/168079b434

CoE (2015a) *Mirrors: Manual on Combating Antigypsyism Through Human Rights Education*, Strasbourg: CoE.

CoE (2015b) *Roma Youth Participation in Action*, Strasbourg: CoE.

CoE (2016) 'Guidelines for implementation of the Roma Youth Action Plan 2016–2020', Strasbourg: CoE, https://rm.coe.int/CoERMPublicCommonSearchServices/DisplayDCTMConten t?documentId=09000016806abde5

Daróczi, A., Kóczé, A., Jovanovic, C.S., Vajda, V., Kurtic, V., Serban, A. and Smith, L. (2018) 'Gender, ethnicity and activism: "The miracle is when we don't give up …', *Journal of Poverty and Social Justice*, 26(1): 77–94.

Donnelly, J. (2007) 'The relative universality of human rights', *Human Rights Quarterly*, 29(2): 281–306.

End, M. (2012) 'History of antigypsyism in Europe: The social causes', in Phiren Amenca (ed) *The European Boogie Man Complex. Challenging Antigypsism Through Non Formal Education*, Budapest: Phiren Amenca/Council of Europe, https://phirenamenca.eu/the-european-boogie-man-complex-educational-toolkit/

Equality and Human Rights Commission (2018) 'Developing a national barometer of prejudice and discrimination in Britain', Research Report 119, www.equalityhumanrights.com/sites/default/files/national-barometer-of-prejudice-and-discrimination-in-britain.pdf

ERRC (European Roma Rights Centre) (2017) 'Is the EU Roma Framework floundering? Commission reports patchy progress, limited impact and rising racism', 4 September, http://www.errc.org/news/is-the-eu-roma-framework-floundering-commission-reports-patchy-progress-limited-impact-and-rising-racism

European Commission (2018) 'European youth guarantee', http://ec.europa.eu/social/main.jsp?catId=1079

European Youth Forum (2014) 'Multiple discrimination and young people in Europe', Strasbourg: CoE, https://www.youthforum.org/sites/default/files/publication-pdfs/Multiple-discrimination-and-young-people-in-Europe.pdf

Evans, T. and Ayers, A. (2006) 'In the service of power: The global political economy of citizenship and human rights', *Citizenship Studies*, 10(3): 289–308.

EWL (European Women's Lobby) (2012) 'The price of austerity: The impact on women's rights and gender equality in Europe', Belgium: EWL, https://www.womenlobby.org/IMG/pdf/the_price_of_austerity_-_web_edition.pdf

FRA (Fundamental Rights Agency) (2013) 'Analysis of FRA Roma survey results by gender', European Union Agency for Fundamental Rights.

Freire, P. (1972) *Pedagogy of the Oppressed*, Harmondsworth: Penguin.

Gosavi, S. (2016) 'Postcolonial critique of human rights', *Contemporary Research in India*, 6(4): 60–4.

Gov.UK (2017) 'Race disparity audit. Summary findings from the ethnicity facts and figures website', www.gov.uk/government/publications/race-disparity-audit

Gov.UK (2020) 'Strengthening police powers to tackle unauthorised encampments', www.gov.uk/government/consultations/strengthening-police-powers-to-tackle-unauthorised-encampments

Ife, J. and Fiske, L. (2006) 'Human rights and community work: Complementary theories and practices', *International Social Work*, 49(3): 297–308.

Jovanović, J. and Daróczi, A. (2015) 'Still missing intersectionality: The relevance of feminist methodologies in the struggle for the rights of Roma', *Roma Rights*, 2: 79–82.

Jovanović, J., Kóczé, A. and Balogh, L. (2015) *Intersections of Gender, Ethnicity, and Class: History and Future of the Romani Women's Movement*, Budapest: Central European University.

Labour Party (2017) 'Manifesto: For the many not the few', London: LP, https://labour.org.uk/wp-content/uploads/2017/10/labour-manifesto-2017.pdf

Lorde, A. (1984) 'The master's tools will never dismantle the master's house', in *Sister Outsider: Essays and Speeches*, New York, NY: The Crossing Press, pp 110–14, https://collectiveliberation.org/wp-content/uploads/2013/01/Lorde_The_Masters_Tools.pdf

McGarry, A. (2014) 'Roma as a political identity: Exploring representations of Roma in Europe', *Race and Class*, 14(6): 756–74.

Phiren Amenca (2016) *Volunteering – Citizens' Tools for Roma Participation*, Budapest: Phiren Amenca.

Roma Rights Defenders (2018) 'Join us', www.errc.org/get-involved/join-us

Sen, A. (1999) *Development as Freedom*, Oxford: Oxford University Press.

Simhandl, K. (2006) '"Western Gypsies and Travellers"–"Eastern Roma": The creation of political objects by the institutions of the European Union', *Nations and Nationalism*, 12(1): 97–115.

Tišer, D. (2015) 'Human Dimension Implementation Meeting Warsaw, 21 September to 2 October 2015. Working session 16 Tišer tolerance and non-discrimination Roma and Sinti issue, including: Implementation of the OSCE Action Plan on Improving the Situation of Roma and Sinti', www.osce.org/odihr/188136?download=true

Traveller Pride (2019) https://www.lgbttravellerpride.com/

Travellers' Times (2016) 'Lisa Smith says government need to think again about gypsy status', www.travellerstimes.org.uk/features/lisa-smith-says-government-need-think-again-about-gypsy-status

Travellers' Times (2018a) 'Home page', www.travellerstimes.org.uk/

Travellers' Times (2018b) 'Young Gypsies and Travellers launch activist network at Appleby Fair', www.travellerstimes.org.uk/news/2018/06/young-gypsies-and-travellers-launch-activist-network-appleby-fair

Trehan, N. (2009) 'Human rights entrepreneurship in post-Socialist Hungary: From "Gypsy problem" to "Romani rights"', PhD thesis, London School of Economics.

UNICEF (United Nations Children's Fund) (2018) 'Youth empowerment', www.unicef.org/innovation/innovation_91018.html

United Nations (2018) 'End of mission statement of the Special Rapporteur on Contemporary Forms of Racism, Racial Discrimination, Xenophobia and Related Intolerance at the conclusion of her mission to the United Kingdom of Great Britain and Northern Ireland', www.ohchr.org/EN/NewsEvents/Pages/DisplayNews.aspx?NewsID=23073&LangID=E

Yuval-Davis, N. (1999) 'What is "transversal politics"?', *Soundings*, 12: 94–8.

Yuval-Davis, N. (2014) *Human Security and the Gendered Politics of Belonging*, Warwick: Social Sciences, Centre for the Study of Women and Gender, https://warwick.ac.uk/fac/soc/sociology/research/centres/gender/calendar/pastevents/symposium/yuval/

Zimmerman, M. (1990) 'Taking aim on empowerment research: On the distinction between individual and psychological conceptions', *American Journal of Community Psychology*, 18(1): 169–77.

SEVEN

Transatlantic dialogues and the solidarity of the oppressed: critical race activism in the US and Canada

Nidhi Trehan and Margareta Matache

Introduction

As a growing number of Central and East European Roma progressively became European Union (EU) citizens, Romani people, activists, scholars and their allies nurtured a hope that the systemic inequalities that haunted Romani communities for centuries would finally be dismantled. However, although progress can be observed in European policies (at least on paper), national strategies vis-à-vis Roma or even enrolment rates in primary education, the complex and intertwined problems of unaddressed historical injustice, economic injustice, exclusion and anti-Romani racism continue to this day.

Few gains have been achieved, even in relation to ensuring the basic right of Romani children to access quality education as segregation in schools remains a shameful reality in many EU member states. Indeed, a recent EU report indicates that the school segregation rate for Romani children across Europe actually increased from 10 per cent in 2011 to 15 per cent in

2016 (FRA, 2018). For Romani children, school enrolment clearly does not equal access to quality, non-discriminatory education. Moreover, in countries such as Hungary and Poland, the neoliberal politics of the post-transition decades have been replaced by a corrosive politics of populism and resurgent ethno-nationalism (see Chapter One).

Although Romani self-organizing dates back to the early 1900s in Europe, activism in the US has long held great relevance for the Romani movement. The US civil rights movement and strategic litigation were models for the fledgling post-socialist Romani movement in Europe as it began to revive, expand and strengthen in the early 1990s. Euro-Atlantic integration, via institutions such as the Council of Europe, North Atlantic Treaty Organization (NATO) and the EU, reinforced liberal conceptions of rights, and a neoliberal view of the role of civil society increasingly took hold. In response, disillusioned by weak and biased 'integration' processes (including National Roma Integration Strategies) that did little to address socio-economic exclusion, some Romani activists and scholars have turned to calling on governments to focus on structural anti-Romani racism. Moreover, Romani activists were influenced by critical North American debates on effective community organizing and mobilization, including how movements can be derailed through donor-driven agendas (Trehan, 2001).

This chapter explores the relationship between European and North American Romani activism through the experiences and reflections of Margareta 'Magda' Matache, a Romanian Romani activist and scholar who is Director of the Roma Program at Harvard University's FXB Center, and Nidhi Trehan, a political sociologist engaged in the movement for the rights of Romani peoples since the mid-1990s. We also incorporate the Roma-related advocacy work of Serbian-Canadian Roma based in Montreal, Quebec, primarily that of Dafina Savić, a human rights activist and founder of the non-governmental organization Romanipe, and the journalist Lela

Savić, as well as activists within Voice of Roma, a Roma-led organization based in San Francisco.

The first section of this chapter is based on a dialogic interview between us that offers a window into contemporary Romani activism, which increasingly employs an anti-racist, intersectional approach that seeks to highlight voices and approaches hitherto neglected. The second section provides case studies of transatlantic Romani activism today in the US and Canada, and draws lessons learned on recognition battles, anti-racist work and its reparatory potential on the frayed social contract between the state and the (Romani) citizen.

Throughout these discussions, it became clear to us that contemporary transatlantic Romani activists – those who have crossed over from Europe to North America – have a distinct perspective on these critical issues, and that Reverend King's 'fierce urgency of now' continues apace for the global Romani justice movement.

Reflections on Romania and the work of Romani CRISS

With a long history in Romani activism and advocacy work with the Roma Centre for Social Intervention and Studies (Romani CRISS [RC]), Magda has engaged with the European Romani movement and EU policy since the late 1990s, and is active in advocacy work with the US Congress on Roma recognition as well. Thus, we discuss her insights into the pitfalls, gains and enduring lessons within Romani organizing, strategy and anti-racist work.

This section is semi-biographical, and through Magda's journey in Romani activism, we see resonances with the narratives of many Romani activists who grew up in the time of profound transition in Central and Eastern Europe when countries in the region challenged communism from the late 1980s onwards, setting a course to becoming liberal democracies and joining the EU and NATO. However, the transition in the 1990s also meant absorption into neoliberal economies, where austerity measures and 'restructuring' led to growing unemployment, social insecurity and rising violence against Romani people unleashed by acute ethno-nationalist forces. Magda recalls growing up in the shadow of the terrible anti-Romani pogroms in Hadareni and Kogalniceanu in early 1990s' Romania, when mobs burnt down the homes of Roma (ERRC, 1996: 6–7). At one point, her father mediated a potentially violent attack against Roma in her hometown in Ilfov County with the help of leaders from Bucharest, and she recalls being frightened for her father's safety and by the palpable threat of the attack.

In 1999, as a social work student at the University of Bucharest, Magda began working with RC, a leading Romani rights organization, to help obtain documents and birth certificates for families in the Romani neighbourhood of Zabrauti (Bucharest), enabling them to access their rights as citizens (a common challenge for many Roma). Then, in 2001, Nicoleta Bitu became Magda's mentor at RC: "I owe a lot to Nicoleta ... she introduced me to the world of tactics on how to create resources and power within Romani communities, especially with Romani women and youth." From this point on, she also worked with the late Nicolae Gheorghe, a sociologist and the founder of RC, and a pioneering Romani activist, policymaker and institution builder in Romania and internationally. At the end of 2005, she became the Executive Director of RC, continuing in this role until 2012. Here, she reflects on some of her successes:

'Our work focused primarily on documenting cases of discrimination and abuse of Roma. We looked at violations of human rights against Roma and brought cases to court, and employed test case litigation to eventually render change in legislation and policy. So, it was a very straightforward path, partially inspired by American struggles on public school segregation and the use of case law. We also focused on creating

Romani leadership and power in communities, including health mediators and human rights monitors. And it partially worked!'

In 2005, RC urged the Ministry of Education (MoE) to adopt a law on recognizing education segregation as a discriminatory phenomenon based on a pattern of discrimination that Romani children faced in Romania. RC then worked to build a strong coalition with Amare Romentza, and two *gadje*-led organizations – The Intercultural Centre in Timisoara and OvidiuRo – to join forces on desegregation and intercultural learning. The coalition received Office of Security and Cooperation in Europe (OSCE) support as Nicolae Gheorghe was Head of the Contact Point for Sinti & Roma at the time. Ultimately, a partnership was formed between the NGO coalition and the MoE, who agreed on a memorandum for working jointly on segregation in state schools and intercultural education. In 2007, the MoE adopted an ordinance that prohibited segregation in education, and another one promoting intercultural education and diversity.

RC staff felt that although the drafting of policy, the partnership with other NGOs, the tactics employed and the advocacy work were all successful, regrettably, there was little change on the ground. Magda adds:

'Another moment of hope on desegregation and equal access to education came in 2011 when our Parliament amended the Education Act to prohibit placement in special schools on ethnic grounds. To implement the amendment, RC collaborated with MPs along with Romani leaders, such as Petre-Florin Manole (now an MP with the Social Democratic Party), Amare Romentza and allies. We personally approached the Parliamentary committee drafting this law. Still, the only point which the committee adopted was recognizing the abuse of school placements on ethnic grounds of children in special schools, as one of the parliamentarians was especially sensitive to this issue, and the other points were left out of the national Education Act.'

As seen earlier, these desegregation initiatives, as in other parts of Europe, had limited success as they were unable to overcome institutional racism (see also Matache and Barbu, 2018). Another observation of Roma policymakers and activists – both during the time of transition and the present day – is that they only have a limited say as they are often silenced or not heard. Racist behaviour, paternalism and, at best, tokenism, as well as a corrosive one-upmanship, are far too common. Magda reflects on how this has prompted her own anti-racist work rooted in Romani representation, and weaves it into a broader conversation on the role of Romani people in spaces and places of power:

'Perhaps in the past few years, we have seen some seeds of hope in the representation of Roma in a few governments, parliaments and intergovernmental organizations. *But, as a people, I would say we are still lagging behind in terms of representation, leadership and power.* We must be vocal in demanding our place at the table. In the case of other marginalized groups … their leaders and scholars would certainly not stay silent if someone organizes public fora on their oppression, and there isn't enough representation from their particular group. I think in the case of Roma, *gadje* continue to discount us. We continue to see non-Roma represent us and speak on behalf of, or about, us, and even though it may not be the same as the 1990s, this power differential is still there. Often, we don't see a conscious and intentional effort to rectify this.'

Moreover, within the movement, the quest for power and visibility often results in corrosive competition, rather than collaboration based on mutual trust, and we have seen this in the history of Romani and pro-Romani organizations. As Magda acknowledges, RC had a complex relationship with the ERRC:

'Sometimes, we worked well together; other times, we felt they used our work without proper credit and equal partnership. During my mandate at RC, I tried to reconcile our relationship with the ERRC several times but it didn't turn out very well, and I felt that it was because I encountered backlash from a white male Romanian "saviour". It's really hard to have such conversations because it just looks like two organizations fighting for credit and/or visibility when Romani people are struggling with oppression. *Thus, how do we critique this and dismantle the power imbalance? How do we ensure that we practice justice when we promote justice? It's a work in progress, and it's complicated indeed* ... and we lost our chance to experience the power of true partnership and solidarity.'

Despite some progress, a continuing issue is the lack of representation within the staff of many pro-Romani or human rights organizations, and Nidhi shares her insights:

'As an Indian-American, I felt like I had a very different perspective on working within the ERRC in 1996. I had already been to Shuto Orizari (one of the largest Romani settlements in the world), and met Bulgarian Roma communities and activists before coming to Budapest. It was my first full-time job after my master's degree in public policy, and I was very passionate about our mission at the ERRC. I was the only person of colour there at the time and, often, I would ask in staff meetings, "When are we going to hire Roma? When?" And after some time, we had some Romani interns ... but it's not the same thing. Nicolae Gheorghe was on our board (and, later, Hristo Kyuchukov and Rudko Kawcyznski) but having

Romani staff persons who work in operations and who set the priorities was very important to me – *indeed, all the knowledge was within the Romani communities themselves.* But it also seemed that Nicolae couldn't push the power structure to hire Roma fast enough. This was my main problem with the European *Roma* Rights Centre, where are the Roma I would ask? It was frustrating and I left after only two years there. Afterwards, the ERRC gradually hired Roma full-time staff (first Angela Kóczé, and then others). So, the criticisms I raised back then began to be addressed little by little.'

Today, the ERRC, with a Romani leadership and staff representation, continues to be a lead civil society actor in the arena of Romani rights.

Differences in ideas, philosophies and solutions on human rights work among Romani activists are contentious issues that Magda has long grappled with. Coming to the US was transformative for her thinking, and she elaborates on the journey from RC to Harvard:

'When I led Romani CRISS, sometimes, certain leaders around us felt that we were too "inclusive". Once, when RC joined the LGBT [lesbian, gay, bisexual and trans] Pride March in Bucharest, I faced some adverse reactions from a well-known leader in the movement. And there were many moments when I made particular choices against the stream, and I faced backlash from other Romani leaders … which was fine. Sometimes, my political choices upset others. Often, I made mistakes; and other times, I got things right. But my heart was always in the right place for Romani people.

Also, while Nicolae Gheorghe had a strong influence on my growth through his ideas on human rights and movement building, we also had disagreements. When I became the Director of RC, one issue we disagreed on was the fact that Nicolae was trying to question and conceptualize if and when Romani activists needed to recognize the role of some Romani communities in the predicament of their destitution. For instance, he wanted RC to get involved in work on begging – to denounce it, to speak out against begging as a practice amongst some Roma communities – as he was wondering whether it was our duty as Roma to do this for Roma.

But I had a different opinion. Back then, I thought that "No, it's not for us to deal with the failures of the state; it's the role of the state to repair the harm and the exploitation of Roma dating back to slavery and to support Roma pushed into begging, not to blame them." The media too presented begging as a Romani cultural issue, as if begging was somehow part of "Romani culture". Thus, I was not willing to contribute to the growth of that racist idea. I didn't entertain it then, and I don't entertain it now; but now I understand that it's because I embrace more of an anti-racist school of thought. So, Nicolae and us, the team at RC, we fought over these issues, and our paths diverged. Some activists portray our separation as a fight for power but it was mostly based on philosophical differences, although we continued to share the same goal and hope for Roma justice.'

Magda also relates a contemporary schism within the movement arising from the responses to the COVID-19 pandemic:

'In April 2020, a few communities in Romania became visible in the national media due to police violence perpetrated against them, as well as a conflict between two rival families. The first thing some Romani activists did back home was to apologize on social media and television for the alleged "misconduct of Roma". To me, that felt like an "assimilationist" mindset by definition

[Kendi, 2016]. More importantly, I felt that they should have spoken to the people beaten up by the police *before* they blamed and mocked them. *And I do think that we have to break out of these patterns, which show how we Roma, too, internalize white supremacist ideas.* It was only when I came to Harvard that I began to articulate and verbalize my critical race perspective, for example, my take on "racecraft" [Fields and Fields, 2014] or the ideology of criminality that pathologizes and demonizes Romani people to justify oppression. I have embraced ideas of anti-racism, justice and reparation as solutions for Roma, and these are beyond the individual human rights framework.

I have been influenced by the work of African-American thinkers, in particular, Kendi, a theorist on the racial state and racial disparities in the US. In *Stamped from the Beginning* [Kendi, 2016], he suggests there are three different perspectives on racial disparities, each embodied by people with distinct attitudes. The first are the *anti-racists*, those who talk about racial disparities in an anti-racist framework that focuses on dismantling racism. I believe I now belong to this school of thought. The second are the *assimilationists*, and they see racial disparities, on the one hand, as related to discrimination but they also partially blame or question oppressed people themselves. So, for example, if a policeman kills a Black or Romani person, they would say that "it's bad, but, see, that man was stealing", and so on. The third category Kendi terms *segregationists*, and these are racist people who put the whole blame for racism on the victims of racial disparities themselves. When I read his books, it created more clarity in my mind around the nature of the conflicting ideas we experience in our movement. But back in Romania, it wasn't the reasoning that informed my point of view, but it was just me thinking instinctively "this is not fair. The police can't abuse and kill a human being, regardless of their criminal background. Everyone has a fundamental right to life."

Nevertheless, I still believe that strategic litigation, human rights work and policy advocacy are mandatory for our democracies and Romani individuals and families. So, I believe that the work of RC and other human rights NGOs has been, still is and will remain essential, especially in these times shaken by far-right groups, populists and racists. But I'd say that my work and vision today are focused more on identifying paths to dismantle collective injustices against Roma, anti-racist work and reparations, and an emphasis on the states, societies and the systems of oppression, rather than on "Roma integration". So, while violations of human rights require remedies rooted in individual human rights frameworks, collective injustices require collective remedies. But this is a different moment in our history, in our movement and in my growth as a Romani scholar and activist.'

In her transatlantic work as an activist-scholar based in the US, Magda gains further inspiration from scholars and writers such as Ida B. Wells, W.E.B. Dubois, James Baldwin, Patricia Hill Collins, Cornel West, Barbara Fields, Khalil Gibran Muhammad and many others. These influences have been important in debates on knowledge production and the marginalization of the Romani voice in depictions of Romani life worlds (see Chapter Eight by Kóczé and Trehan). Magda elucidates:

'It was through the work of African-American scholars that I've been emboldened to own my scholarship, and to ignore and not fight against the labels that *gadje* [non-Romani] scholars stamp Roma scholars with (for example, "activist"). *To many of them, we are not scholarly enough, we are not objective enough and, most importantly, we should have stayed where we were 20 years ago – helping them gaining access to our communities.* But I am not going to stop because some want us to stop, or because they feel uncomfortable, or because they feel they are the experts and we are the subjects of their research. There is also a lot to unpack about "*gadjo* objectivity" – and the power of their collective subjectivity – in Roma-related research given that they, too, carry on their shoulders the experiences and legacies of their ancestors – in this case, oppression, enslavement, Holocaust, forced sterilization and so on. And we can all learn from the lessons and struggles of other oppressed people. As you know, the critics of early Black scholarship also called Dubois and others "subjective", "not scholarly enough". And at the same time, we should aspire to gain the courage of Ida B. Wells, whose instrumental work on lynching and dismantling the ideology of criminality paved the way for so many other scholars engaged in the study of racism.'

Reflecting upon her expansive knowledge of human rights work in Romania and other Balkan countries, Magda shares valuable insights on Romani organizing and what skills she built upon in her transatlantic work:

'One thing to note is that whatever we were doing in Romania and with RC, it was not community organizing per se. *It was policy advocacy, strategic litigation, health mediation, human rights work, but it wasn't community organizing.* In a way, strategic litigation has been at the core of many advocacy initiatives of RC and others, inspired as it was, somehow, by the US civil rights movement and the judgment of Oliver Brown vs. the Board of Education of Topeka, Kansas and others in 1954.

However, the Roma movement has yet to make demands for reparations, to work towards economic or environmental justice, and to build power through community organizing and mobilization, protest, and mass action. Up to this day,

I cannot point to many genuine instances of community organizing as such in Romani communities. There are some initiatives in Romania and other parts of Europe but they are far from fitting into the framework of real organizing. But there is some hope as seeds of community organizing have recently been sown in North Macedonia.'

For Magda, à la Ganz (2013/14), *community organizing means the creation of power within communities.* In fact, community leadership can greatly strengthen the work of NGOs. She hastens to add that the 'NGO advocacy' model that is now seen in Europe is not wrong; it is just one approach among a diversity of tactics within human rights work. Creating NGOs and establishing goals towards policy advocacy or case law continues to be valuable. She suggests some new pathways for organizing:

'Successful social movements in Europe, such as Serbia on the Move,[1] are making an effort to build leadership and the power of the people within local communities, be they parents, patients or, broadly, citizens. Yet, Roma and pro-Roma NGOs in Europe have focused primarily on litigation, service provision projects and advocacy work. And while their efforts have shown some results, organizing Romani parents, youths and adults with lived experiences of segregation in special schools has been tried in only a few places. Miroslav Klempar and the Awen Amenca team in Czech Republic are using this approach [Prague Monitor, 2020]. *I argue that most "organizing efforts" have not invested in, and therefore have not created, the power and organizing skills of the people. Meanwhile, human rights NGOs are losing their efficacy due to lack of funding and pressure from governments, so there is currently a serious void in advocacy and desegregation tactics.'*

As mentioned earlier, Magda cites the influence of the strategic organizing philosophy of scholar-activist Marshall Ganz of

Harvard's Kennedy School. In his youth, Ganz had been a volunteer with the 1964 Mississippi Summer Project, and then an organizer for the Student Nonviolent Coordinating Committee (SNCC), a youth focused civil rights group working in the South. In the autumn of 1965, he joined Cesar Chavez and Dolores Huerta in an effort to unionize California's farm workers, and later, through his academic research, was able to fuse activism with knowledge production and generate a novel approach to organizing. Magda explains:

> 'Let me be clear, in the Roma movement, we've seen some NGOs trying to implement community organizing projects but, unfortunately, the tactics did not lead to a shift in power towards the people and, thus, sustainable constituencies were never built. And when I say "constituency", I use Ganz's [2013/14] definition, namely, "A community organized to use its resources to act on behalf of their own interests." We are all accustomed to a model in which mostly national-level activists and NGOs voice the Roma-related concerns of local communities. *A power over* as opposed to a *power with* model, as Ganz would say. This is not to say that there aren't any challenges in organizing actual constituencies, nor that community organizing is the panacea in dismantling anti-Romani racism, but it is to say that there is power in building strong constituencies with a base at the local level. And organizing could be an effective tool.'

Magda offers her perspectives on the critical importance of local organizing as a bulwark against the vagaries of top-down government policies:

> 'Based on my own mistakes and experiences, I think it is essential. It gives more power to people because then they don't depend on donors, and can't be put down by the government easily. I experienced first-hand how the

government put down Romani CRISS, in a moment when we were at a crossroads: either implement desegregation together with state schools ourselves *or* let the harmful phenomenon persist. We decided to partner with the MoE and one hundred schools on desegregation. And though these were state schools (under the MoE) implementing the desegregation activities, the MoE decided not to reimburse the costs for materials, which were considerable over two to three years. And although they initially approved 90 per cent of our work and expenses, later the state bureaucracy blocked us. Their decision was based on an unfounded "suspicion" of key activities not being implemented, although they were conducted by their own local bodies, that is, the state schools. This problem hasn't been resolved since 2012, and RC is still fighting them in court and even after several recent positive decisions from the courts in Romania, as thousands of reports and pictures from the schools implementing the project prove the MoE wrong. We received a lot of political pressure and mistreatment from the MoE.

Community organizing has a better chance to be sustainable in the long run because it doesn't depend on a call for proposals from a donor, but on the needs of local people and the power they generate for themselves. I also think that for Roma, it's not just a matter of violations of individual rights. So, if we are to go into "Western thinking" [liberal human rights framework] about imagining rights, it's a very "white framework" because it was built on the idea that violations are perpetrated predominantly against individuals. *But in the case of racialized minorities, such as Roma, it is also about structural racism, patterns of collective injustice, not just about violations of individual rights. The problems we racialized groups face are structural, so working on an anti-racist agenda is essential for communities of colour since we need to dismantle structural racism.*

Certainly, the individual rights framework remains *mandatory*. It's important to be able to go to court, to be able to point out these patterns of structural discrimination. In the landmark case of education desegregation in Europe, *D.H. v. the Czech Republic (2007)*, as well as in other cases, a few-dozen Romani children did receive remedies after the ECtHR [European Court of Human Rights] judgment found they had been unjustly placed in special schools. However, as Jacqueline and I wrote in our book on reparations [Bhabha and Matache, forthcoming], *does $4000, the amount received by each of the 17 applicants in D.H. v. the Czech Republic, undo the lifelong impact of social, economic and emotional segregation in an educational system with an inferior curriculum?* Moreover, how do we ensure justice and remedies for the large number of Romani children facing similar circumstances? A majority of them cannot go to court. *The ECtHR accepted as evidence, and consequently as true, statistics showing the structural nature of segregation and demanded policy changes. But how do we ensure reparatory justice for collective injustice?'*

Magda emphasizes the need for shifting strategy and making specific demands beyond a mere call for the acknowledgement of racism and the need for racial justice, suggesting the requirement for focused approaches to tackle structural problems:

'I believe we need a strong advocacy movement that focuses on structural racism, wealth and resource inequalities, *and* on reparations. Much of our work at Harvard focuses on reparations, and we started collaborating with Romani advocates and scholars to emphasize the issue of reparations in knowledge production, advocacy and policy demands. We are also contributing to the strengthening of a global conversation and a coalitional advocacy movement on reparations claims across historical and geographical spaces. Most importantly, we have set out several reparations strategies that are relevant in addressing the continuum of Roma collective injustices in Europe: (a) truth-telling; (b) memorializing resistance; (c) victim empowerment; (d) offender accountability; (e) restitution; (f) apology; (g) reparative compensation; and (h) legal measures [see Matache and Bhabha, 2020].'

Magda also reflects on how to build coalitions and the value of intersectional alliances with other marginalized groups:

'What I learned in the US is that solidarity work takes a lot of effort and patience. In my work here at Harvard, including with Black Americans and Dalit people, first of all, what we are trying to do is to create friendships between our struggles. We are trying to understand each other, learn the history of the specific forms of oppression we face, the vocabulary we use in each movement, and support each other [a basis for building trust in each other]. It's a slower process but sensitive to the specificities of each group and more sustainable in the longer term.'

Notably, Magda has developed a close collaborative relationship with Professor Cornel West, a renowned public intellectual and teacher on race and social justice at Harvard, and in a 2018 piece in *The Guardian*, they discuss the historical wrongs perpetrated on their peoples:

The impetus to kill and chain Roma and African American bodies remains one of the appalling facets of how the criminalization and demonization of these peoples have historically translated into action.... From early on in their histories, Roma and African Americans crossed similar paths, as white policymakers continued to employ similar tactics to maintain white normativity, social power, and privilege. (Matache and West, 2018)

Alongside West, Magda has been engaged in dialogue with Suraj Yengde, a Dalit scholar at Harvard, on solidarities between communities of colour and bridge-building between African-Americans, Dalits and Roma, and has been an interlocutor, along with Angela Kóczé, in Harvard debates on solidarity strategies, as well as the feminist of colour panel discussions with African-American, Dalit, Palestinian and Romani feminists. Here, a key goal is to forge solidarity networks with other oppressed minority groups, and our discussion raised the significance of creating an inter-community 'safe place' where you are free to contemplate on the oppression and anxiety you face, even in the midst of building a coalition:

'With reference to "safe places", often, the level of understanding of pain and harm in scholars belonging to historically oppressed groups is stronger, so I feel safer in having these conversations and learning from others. For me, it has been harder to build coalitions with some white feminists as it's been frustrating the way in which some white feminists want to engage with Romani feminism. Some want to focus on intra-community issues, such as early marriages, while we believe their voices would have greater impact on issues of intersectional discrimination and racism, and on discrepancies in access to education, health and jobs between Roma and non-Romani women. But while that would have been more helpful for us, it would have been more uncomfortable for them. Romani scholarship and activism are not as mature as in other movements. For decades, we have borrowed and adjusted tactics from the US and other civil rights movements. We also adopted concepts and vocabulary from Black American scholarship – and thousands of books have been written in this area, whereas with

Roma, we are still at the beginning, and much of the scholarship has been written by non-Roma. *I believe that while we learn from other groups, we also need to keep in mind the specificities of our history and our people.*'

Here, Nidhi emphasizes the importance of solidarity work among a diversity of groups, and reflects on racism in the US and her motivation for working in the field:

'Professor Ian Hancock was a key influence upon me, and taking his course on "Gypsy Language and Culture" in 1992 at the University of Texas at Austin greatly inspired me to learn about Roma and their human rights situation. Hancock, as my mentor, emphasized: "If you want to understand Roma, you'll have to go to Europe." And so I worked as a human rights researcher at the ERRC in the mid-1990s, just as the Roma movement was becoming "formalized" with the emergence of "Roma rights" NGOs in Central Eastern Europe. Part of my desire to get involved stemmed from my own experiences of racism in the US. When my family immigrated from India to the US in the 1970s, the "N-word" was still a term of abuse used by white racists, and I experienced it myself as a child in Ohio. In Europe, as I began working with Roma and learning the Romani language, I discovered further connections between Romani culture and that of my birthplace, thereby embracing a broader understanding of "diaspora".'

Magda also reflects upon the early days of the programme at Harvard with Professor Bhabha, the Director of Research at the FXB Center:

'I first met Jackie in 2010 when she came to Romania and wanted to conduct participatory action research (PAR) with local Roma. Jackie and Arlan Fuller

(FXB Center's director then) wanted to establish PAR initiatives with young people. At that time, RC was working with the International Research & Exchanges Board [IREX] on project development and identifying community needs with high school students, so it was a good fit with Harvard's goals. Then, once I joined as a postdoctoral fellow in 2012, I suggested we organize the first of what was to become an "Annual Roma Conference" at Harvard, with the financial support of the OSCE (via Andrejz Mirga). In the first year of the conference in 2013, eminent panellists attended, including Nobel Prize-winning economist Amartya Sen and Jack Greenberg, a respected white American lawyer who had worked on *Brown v. Board of Education*, and is also a friend of RC.'

PAR gives those being researched a central role in the design of research, the collection of data and its interpretation, and ideally leads to change in their lives, as Magda explains: "Our participatory methodology challenged conventional Roma-related research, both in terms of structure (top-down, paternalistic research 'on' Roma) and focus, that is, the tendency to view obstacles to educational advancement particularly through the lens of economic deprivation and Roma 'vulnerability'."

Another project that Magda and Jackie are coordinating, along with Voice of Roma, a transatlantic Romani advocacy group established in 1996 by Sani Rifati that promotes Romani culture, is 'The Romani Realities in the US' study, which sheds light on key aspects of Romani-American life. It covers education, discrimination by law enforcement and identity issues, such as language and the ethnonyms American Roma prefer (that is, 'Roma', 'G★psy', 'Romani people'). It promises to be path-breaking for the US because scholarship on American Roma written in the 1970s/80s was generally limited to anthropological works on particular communities.

The Harvard/Voice of Roma study gives an overview of the contemporary situation of Roma across the US, raising issues of discrimination of Romani people based on ethnicity. One Romani-American entrepreneur familiar with the study offered us his perspective on its significance in June 2020:

'It will have positive influences in two specific areas: access to education and to economic schemes for minority businesses. For too long, we have been labelled as being part of so-called criminal gangs. Some states still have "Gypsy Task force" police who monitor and racially profile us. When we go out to work as contractors (in construction and related trades) – and understand that 95 per cent of us are self-employed and small business owners – they often shut down our work, arrest us and, sometimes, we even get jail sentences for up to 20 years. So, if the study helps to show that we are an ethnic minority, I'm hoping we will no longer be seen as "criminal gangs", but as a genuine ethnic group in America, and be eligible for the government's minority-owned business tax breaks in the future. And we would qualify for education scholarships too.'

Indeed, this could have a profound impact on how Romani people are perceived within US society, and plant the seed for rectifying centuries of mistrust and discrimination, as Romani-Americans would finally be part of the 'American mosaic' as a people whose culture and economic contributions are recognized and valued across society.

Advocacy in focus: Romani activists go to Washington and Ottawa

This section covers two parallel efforts on the recognition of Roma in North America. The first effort is that of the 'DC Working Group', which consists of a core group of Romani people and allies in the US, including: Magda; Nathan Mick, an

American Romanichal based in Kentucky who was previously a congressional aide and is active in Republican Party circles; Erika Schlager, counsellor-at-law with the Conference on Security and Cooperation in Europe (CSCE)/Helsinki Commission (she has been actively following Romani affairs since the 1990s); Jim Goldston, a legal advocate and director of the Open Society Institute's Justice Initiative; Professor Ethel Brooks, who, until recently, represented Roma and Sinti at the US Holocaust Memorial Council and is herself a transatlantic activist and scholar; Dr Petra Gelbart, a Czech-American Romani activist; Jud Nirenberg and David Meyers of the US State Department; and Kristin Raeesi and Professor Carol Silverman, activists with the Voice of Roma.[2] Initially, in the DC Working Group, Magda proposed a resolution to recognize an annual 'Roma Heritage Month' but, ultimately, the group decided pragmatically on a congressional resolution for the recognition of Romani American heritage and International Roma Day (8 April), the Romani Holocaust Memorial (2 August) and the slavery of Roma.

The next stage was the most crucial one, that of lobbying congressional leaders and gaining their sponsorship. American Rom Nathan Mick worked to enlist bipartisan support for the Bill, and was able to get several co-sponsors from the Republican Party, such as Representative Steve Watkins of Kansas and Senator Roger Wicker of Missouri. Representatives Alcee L. Hastings (D–FL), Steve Watkins (R–KS) and Andy Barr (R–KY) introduced H.Res.292, Celebrating the heritage of Romani Americans, a resolution that marks 8 April 2019 as International Roma Day, honours the culture, history and heritage of the Romani people, and raises awareness of the widespread human rights abuses and discrimination that Romani people continue to face. Senator Benjamin Cardin (Democrat from Maryland) and Senator Roger Wicker (Republican from Mississippi) introduced Senate Resolution 141, A Resolution Celebrating the heritage of Romani Americans, on 4 April 2019.

Congressional leaders Hastings, Watkins, Wicker and Cardin issued the following statement:

> Roma enrich the fabric of our nation. They have been part of every wave of European migration to the United States since the colonial period, tying our country to Europe and building the transatlantic bond. Through this resolution, we celebrate our shared history and applaud the efforts to promote transnational cooperation among Roma at the historic First World Romani Congress on April 8, 1971. (US House of Representatives, 2019)

Further advocacy efforts in Congress were coordinated by Victoria Rios, an American Romani activist from a renowned Flamenco music family in Spain, who spearheaded a letter-writing campaign supporting the adoption of the resolution. Activists and scholars, including from Voice of Roma, and other American and European Romani people, also participated. The resolution is yet to be adopted by the US Congress.

With respect to Canada, it is critical to point out the common roots of structural racism with its neighbour to the south. Black Canadian writer Desmond Cole elucidates:

> They are both countries dominated by settler colonial white governments and white majority populations. They are both places that displaced and killed Indigenous people to take their land. And so the legacies of colonialism are the same in both countries – not identical, but those legacies carry on in our institutions today. And just like the US, our police forces were designed to do these things – to catch slaves who were running away, to push Indigenous peoples off of their territories. And those police functions … and the institutions are the same … giving us the same outcomes you would expect. (NPR, 2020)

The history of modern Romani activism in Canada can be traced to the seminal work of Quebec-born writer, activist and linguist Ronald Lee. In the 1970s, he assisted Romani refugees and migrants from communist regimes in central and eastern Europe as well as Yugoslavia. Along with renowned linguist, scholar and activist Professor Ian Hancock (OBE), American Kalderash Romani leader John Tene and actor Yul Brynner, Lee was an integral part of the International Romani Union (IRU) delegation that successfully petitioned the United Nations in New York City in July 1978 for NGO Status Category III for the IRU; this was granted in 1979, and then upgraded in 1993 to Category II status (Acton, 2017; Lee, 2018).

Then, from 1989 to 1990, he assisted Romani asylum seekers from eastern Europe, going on to establish the Roma Community and Advocacy Centre in Toronto in 1997, as well as the Western Canadian Romani Alliance in Vancouver the subsequent year, leaving behind a rich legacy for a younger generation of Romani-Canadian activists to build upon (Lee, 2018).

Similar to contemporary Romani activism in the US, key issues – such as raising the visibility of the rights of Romani asylum seekers and immigrants to Canada, and the recognition of the Roma Holocaust – have been addressed by Dafina Savić of the NGO Romanipe and professional journalist Lena Savić, both of whom are involved with transatlantic anti-racist work from their base in Montreal, Quebec. Dafina Savić, a former United Nations Minority Fellow, in her testimony from 11 June 2019 before the Subcommittee on International Human Rights Committee of the Canadian Parliament, recounts the work of Romanipe[3]:

> Securing rights for Romani refugees has been a priority for us, so the elimination of Bill C-31 … or at least the revision of the criteria used to determine what does and does not constitute a 'safe country' is definitely a priority. I think the Canadian government has the responsibility,

at least as a first step, to speak out about the very gross violations that Roma are facing. When Roma are being killed, the world is actually silent. So, I think Canada could take a lead on responsibility in this. (Government of Canada, 2019, testimony by D. Savić)

Here, she outlines the importance of bridge-building with other oppressed groups in Canada:

Seven years ago, I founded a not-for-profit organization … and [we] built collaborations with many different groups who have been victims of genocide. In the spirit of standing in solidarity, but also in action with those groups, we want to acknowledge our solidarity with people who have presented before this Committee, namely Indigenous peoples as well as the people of Burundi and the Rohingya in Myanmar. (Government of Canada, 2019, testimony by D. Savić)

Dafina Savić then offers her views on Romani persecution in Europe through segregation, extreme poverty and anti-Romani racism, problems exacerbated by the rise of the radical right in recent decades, and that compel many Roma to seek asylum in Canada:

How has the Canadian government reacted to this? Unfortunately, in 2012 under the previous government, a lot of Roma were coming to Canada to seek asylum and seek protection from the rise of the neo-Nazi movement. This was just in 2012, when the far-right reached its peak. Actually, in a village in Hungary, six Roma were killed, including a six-year-old boy, as a result of these attacks by the far-right. A large number of Roma came to Canada to seek asylum. *The response of the government at the time was unfortunately to repeat that rhetoric of criminality, accusing Roma of being bogus refugees undeserving of Canadian protection.* (Government of Canada, 2019, testimony before Parliament by D. Savić. Emphases added)

To European Roma, these actions may seem modest but, in fact, this is path-breaking for North American Romani advocacy because it strengthens the official recognition of Romani people in a part of the world where Roma often survive by being 'invisible' and not drawing attention to themselves. Moreover, the earlier case studies highlight the efficacy of transatlantic Romani organizing and leading national campaigns that mobilize support from US and Canadian lawmakers by combining the synergies of activists in Europe and North America, and are a harbinger for greater collaboration.[4]

Lela Savić, as a journalist and public intellectual, who also leads the Quebec chapter of the Canadian Journalists of Color (CJC),[5] has played an important role in lifting the voices of Romani people in Canada through her community radio initiative and media work. Here, Savić (2019, emphases added) explains the complexities of minority visibility and inclusion within mainstream media:

> *It's not enough to have Romani people enter mainstream media, if you don't change the system, nothing is going to change.* I have an Indigenous friend who is a reporter, and she said, "it's not enough that I'm an Indigenous reporter, because you are putting all the pressure of decolonizing on me, you're putting all the pressure of racism on me.... I entered mainstream media, and now I'm doing conferences on how to decolonize the media".
>
> So, yes, I think it's important that we Roma enter the system, but there is a price to be paid for this, as Fatima Khemilat (2014) suggests. And she cites the French political scientist Jean-Francois Bayart, who says, "dominated people seldom arrive at penetrating the social structures which oppress them". But at what price Khemilat asks?

And she makes a distinction between 'screen' intellectual and 'resistant intellectuals', whereby those who enter the social structures that oppress them, often become a 'screen' of tokenization, thereby reproducing systems of power, while those that resist this tokenization, challenge them. So, the question for Roma is "do you uphold white supremacy or dismantle it?" When you uphold white supremacy, you get rewarded, but when you try to dismantle it, there is a price to be paid.

So, what happens when you have the 'Roma elite' entering the system? What ends up happening is that in order to survive, you will end up *whitening your speech* … so that you don't make the white person feel bad, and that's *white fragility* actually. *White fragility is the idea that white people feel bad all the time whenever you dare to say how oppressed you are, you dare to take up space.* Within Romani studies and Romani activism, are we dismantling white (*gadjo*) supremacy?

The critical race work of Magda Matache, Lela Savić and Dafina Savić points to a new approach within Romani advocacy in North America and internationally, one that places a central emphasis on *positionality* (in terms of Romani 'voice') and *intersectionality* within anti-racist work (see Chapter Eight by Kóczé and Trehan). Within their advocacy, they also harness community initiatives and solidarity building to foster the recognition of Roma at the national policy level – the recognition of both Roma and their struggles within North American political spaces – but also a transatlantic awareness of the struggles of Romani communities back in Europe and those of oppressed groups globally.

The work of anti-racism and intersectional solidarity

Through the rich exchanges between activists, scholars and scholar-activists, we arrive at a few insights as regards the question 'What is to be done?' in terms of dismantling racism and future organizing within the Romani movement. Areas of action include genuine and substantive participation community organizing, cultural representation, and reducing the power differential with *gadje*, as outlined earlier.

The ideas generated from Magda's experience with critical race activism and strategic solidarity development in both Europe and the US – with groups such as African-Americans and Dalits of India – are woven into this narrative of transatlantic Romani activism to highlight the core potential of global anti-racist alliances. Transatlantic activism is enriched by creating diverse coalitions of Roma and other activists of colour to harness the power of intersectional solidarity (the 'together we rise' ethos) for recognition, reparations and anti-racist policies. The synergy and lessons learned from initiatives in Europe and North America take on new significance given the increasingly visible presence of authoritarian (white) nationalist politics in the US, which is further polarizing the citizenry along identity lines.

Regardless of the strategy chosen by activists – organizing, protest, litigation or policy advocacy – they should all become integral parts of the anti-racist tactical repertoire of a coherent and strong Romani anti-racist movement that embraces not only individual rights, but also economic, environmental, social and reparatory justice. In developing a tactical repertoire, the global context needs to be considered. In the summer of 2020, it is evident that President Trump has sought to exploit fears and tensions triggered by the COVID-19 pandemic, the catastrophic economic downturn and structural racism, all in an effort to galvanize his base in order to win re-election in November 2020.

Yet, in response, a diverse and transformational anti-racist movement is also growing. Institutionalized racism, as reflected in the brutal murders of African-Americans Breonna Taylor and George Floyd at the hands of police, spawned a series of Black Lives Matter (BLM) solidarity demonstrations across the globe (Younge, 2020). Roma active in civil society are emphasizing the direct relevance of the BLM movement as a model for Roma to organize against police brutality against Roma (including murders) over the past few years in Europe (Romea.cz, 2020).

Moreover, during the COVID-19 pandemic crisis, activists in Europe point out that racists and nationalists have begun to resort to violent, supremacist tactics. As Matache, Leaning and Bhabha (2020) argue:

> In the past two months, from Ukraine to Spain, Romania, Bulgaria, Slovakia and Serbia, state representatives, police, journalists, and public figures have propagated inflammatory rhetoric, labelling Roma as sources of coronavirus contamination. Bulgaria has instituted discriminatory roadblocks and police checkpoints to target Roma individuals; in Romania, some local stores are allegedly prohibiting the entry of Roma. They all exploit a false narrative to disseminate irrational fear: Roma are transmitters of the virus.

Thus, perhaps one of the most important and immediate points of intersection and solidarity between the US and Europe is the fight for anti-racist policies and against white supremacist nationalism. Today, a new generation of critical Romani activists and thinkers in Europe are exploring ideas centred on intersectionality and structural racism, and wonder what lessons may be learned from similar approaches that groups like BLM (established in 2013) are taking.

However, a remarkable dissonance can be found in the responses of some European leaders who, while pointing out flaws in the US system, hasten to praise Europe for its social inclusion. Margaritis Schinas, the Vice President of the European Commission, stated that Europe had better systems for social inclusion, protection and universal health care than the US (Barigazzi, 2020). He also claimed that:

> there is also a European tradition for protection of minorities, we have less issues than they have in the [United] States…. [This] doesn't mean that we don't have some way still to go in terms of fostering equality and inclusion, income distribution – all these are issues that Europe has still to address. (Barigazzi, 2020)

Such assessments of the treatment of minority groups in Europe are simply not true; rather, they are rather illusory (Barigazzi, 2020). Moreover, such statements underplay or refuse to acknowledge the reality of structural anti-Romani racism in Europe as underscored earlier – particularly during these troubled but transformational times – raising concerns about Europe's commitment to repudiate the current trajectory of white supremacist nationalism in the US.

Nonetheless, there are a few positive signs towards recognizing structural racism in Europe. In June 2020, Ursula von der Leyen, the President of the European Commission, endorsed a discussion on racism within the College of the EU Commission, and stated: "Because each of us has a role to play. This starts with examining ourselves, our unconscious biases and the privileges that we take for granted." In addition, the European Parliament adopted a resolution on the anti-racism protests following the death of George Floyd, indicating a renewed desire to tackle racism and discrimination within Europe itself (European Parliament, 2020).

The work of transatlantic Romani activists and interlocutors based in North America represents a sea change in the movement, with clear positions on intersectionality and solidarity but also an unwavering courage in challenging racist discourses and norms wherever they encounter them. They are engaging in a critique of structural racism and the responses to it, and this presents a far greater challenge to the status quo.

Today, Roma, minority ethnic groups and other minority groups, such as the LGBTQI community and the differently abled, as well as those who believe in democracy, are engaged in an epic and monumental battle against racism. We live in critical times but can also seek inspiration from a new generation of Romani public intellectuals in the US and Europe who believe in anti-racist work and fight and hope for anti-racist societies and policies.

Notes

[1] See: http://en.srbijaupokretu.org/who-are-we/

[2] See: http://www.voiceofroma.com/

[3] For more on Romanipe's activities, see: https://romanipe.wordpress.com/

[4] Indeed, recent efforts by Romani survivors, organizations and individuals has resulted in the official recognition of the Holocaust of the Romani people by the Government of Canada. August 2 will now be marked as an official day of remembrance, and Canada joins Germany, Hungary, Romania, Poland, the Czech Republic and the EU in officially recognizing the Romani Genocide (the US is yet to do so). August 2 commemorates the day in 1944 when 4,300 Roma and Sinti prisoners who remained in the 'Gypsy camp' inside Auschwitz-Birkenau were brutally murdered by Nazis and their collaborators. Recent estimates suggest that across Europe, over 500,000 Roma perished during WWII (https://romanipe.wordpress.com/2020/08/19/a-historical-and-long-awaited-moment-the-government-of-canada-declares-august-2nd-as-an-official-day-of-commemoration-of-the-romani-genocide/).

[5] See: www.cjoc.net

References

Acton, T. (2017) 'Beginnings and growth of transnational movements of Roma to achieve civil rights after the Holocaust', www.romarchive.eu/en/roma-civil-rights-movement/beginnings-and-growth-transnational-movements-roma/

Barigazzi, J. (2020) ' "No doubt" Europe better than US on race issues, EU commissioner says', *Politico*, 10 June, www.politico.eu/article/margaritis-schinas-eu-better-than-us-on-race-issues/?fbclid=IwAR0i02tqTVfFlQs_9c58PaJSU1qQMUCt69O-YgFfZS31S1Tk7m53ucqoXWk

ERRC (European Roma Rights Centre) (1996) 'Sudden rage at dawn: Violence against Roma in Romania', Budapest, Country Reports Series, No. 2, September.

European Parliament (2020) 'Resolution on the anti-racism protests following the death of George Floyd', www.europarl.europa.eu/doceo/document/B-9-2020-0196_EN.html

Fields, K.E. and Fields, B.J. (2014) *Racecraft. The Soul of Inequality in American Life*, London: Verso.

FRA (Fundamental Right Agency) (2018) 'A persisting concern: Anti-Gypsyism as a barrier to Roma inclusion', http://fra.europa.eu/en/publication/2018/roma-inclusion

Ganz, M. (2013/14) 'Organizing: People, power, change', www.hcs.harvard.edu/summercamp/wp-content/uploads/2013/06/What-Is-Organizing-2013.pdf

Government of Canada (2019) 'Subcommittee on International Human Rights Committee', testimony of Dafina Savić, founder and Executive Director of *Romanipe*, 11 June.

Kendi, I.X. (2016) *Stamped from the Beginning: The Definitive History of Racist Ideas in America*, New York: Nation Books.

Khemilat, F. (2014) 'Entre collaboration et résistance: de la délicate position des racisés dans le champ universitaire français', paper presented to the international colloquium on 'L'influence complexe de l'orientalisme dans les discours scientifiques sur l'islam', 11–12 December, UC Berkeley and CADIS-EHESS, CNRS.

Lee, R. (2018) 'The Roma civil rights movement in Canada and the USA', RomArchive, www.romarchive.eu/en/roma-civil-rights-movement/roma-civil-rights-movement-canada-and-usa/

Matache, M. and Barbu, S. (2018) 'A history of school desegregation of Roma' RomArchive, www.romarchive.eu/en/roma-civil-rights-movement/history-school-desegregation-roma/

Matache, M. and Bhabha, J. (forthcoming) 'The Roma case for reparations', in J. Bhabha, M. Matache, C. Elkins and W. Johnson (eds) *Time for Reparation? Addressing State Responsibility for Collective Injustice*, Philadelphia, PA: University of Pennsylvania Press.

Matache, M. and West, C. (2018) 'Roma and African Americans share a common struggle', *The Guardian*, 20 February, www.reuters.com/article/us-hungary-roma-segregation-ruling/hungary-ruling-in-roma-segregation-case-unfair-pm-orban-idUSKBN22R1D5?fbclid=IwAR3WyN9qvA_NsNhilO2VJjPOINhNnbT4DlJgxAgkisp68klRT4YeYBztGoI

Matache, M., Leaning, J. and Bhabha, J. (2020) 'The shameful resurgence of violent scapegoating in a time of crisis', *Open Democracy*, 5 May.

NPR (National Public Radio) (2020) 'Protests spur Canadian activists to confront racism in their own nation', 14 June.

Prague Monitor (2020) 'Roma families see few effects from latest inclusive education reform', http://praguemonitor.com/2020/01/16/be-delivered-roma-still-struggle-receiving-good-education

Romea.cz (2020) 'As US protests continue against police murder, ROMEA recalls 2016 case of Romani man who died in police custody under circumstances like George Floyd', www.romea.cz/en/news/world/as-us-protests-continue-against-police-murder-romea-recalls-2016-case-of-romani-man-who-died-in-police-custody-under

Savić, L. (2019) 'Stigma and Discrimination of Roma in Canada', presentation at 'Neglected Voices: The Global Roma Diaspora', Harvard University, 8 April.

Trehan, N. (2001) 'In the name of the Roma', in W. Guy (ed) *The Roma of Central and Eastern Europe*, Hatfield: University of Hertfordshire Press.

US House of Representatives (2019) 'Resolution 292', https://alceehastings.house.gov/uploadedfiles/bills-116hres292ih.pdf

US Senate (2019) 'Resolution 141', www.congress.gov/bill/116th-congress/senate-resolution/141

Younge, G. (2020) 'What black America means to Europe', *The New Review of Books*, 6 June.

EIGHT

'When they enter, we all enter …': envisioning a New Social Europe from a Romani feminist perspective

Angéla Kóczé and Nidhi Trehan

Introduction

> Epistemic violence, that is, violence exerted against or
> through knowledge, is probably one of the key elements
> in any process of domination. It is not only through the
> construction of exploitative economic links or the control
> of the politico-military apparatuses that domination
> is accomplished, but also, and … most importantly
> through the construction of epistemic frameworks that
> legitimize and enshrine those practices of domination.
> (Galván-Álvarez, 2010)

Romani peoples have been constituted as political subjects
for centuries through forms of epistemic violence, racialized
political and economic exclusion, and cultural erasure. Roma
and their life worlds have almost always been the objects of
non-Romani researchers and scholars; thus, Romani people
have been kept out from the knowledge-making process

themselves. Usually, they have been used exclusively as informants or authentic voices to legitimize non-Romani academic expertise. From the 'Gypsylorist' tradition to the 'benevolent scholars' of today, knowledge of Romani peoples and communities was recorded and interpreted by non-Roma according to the prevailing ideologies and prejudices embedded in their world view. This was symptomatic of the uncritical, unequal power relationship between a people who are studied and those studying them (Matache, 2017).

As this body of knowledge expanded, replete with various stereotypes effectively reproduced over time, the (de-)authorization of Romani knowledge strengthened and contributed to the dehumanization of Roma (see Trehan, 2009). A significant body of academic work on Roma can be classified as what critical race theorist Sylvia Wynter (2003) defines as 'racialization', a classifying mechanism within a hierarchical relationship that identifies social groups as human, subhuman and non-human. Gradually, the stigma attached to Romani identity hardened, and the labelling of Roma as the enduring 'European Other' took hold in the collective *imaginarium* (Lee, 2000).

From a critical perspective, knowledge production on Roma is a classifying mechanism that provides a specific lens and theoretical framework to understand the situation of Roma. One dominant approach in academic knowledge production, favoured by linguists, anthropologists and folklorists, narrowly emphasizes the language distinctiveness and the 'immutable' cultural singularity of Roma as an ethnic group, and this strengthens their racialization (Acton, 2016). Another dominant scholarly approach is the constructivist one, which challenges the narratives of 'Gypsy studies' mentioned earlier and contends that it racializes Roma as non-Europeans (with 'Oriental' origins based on linguistic evidence). Kóczé (2020: 3) explains the limitations of these hegemonic theoretical frameworks, suggesting that both are at some level problematic:

While the first, [the] language and culture-centric approach ([whether] consciously or unconsciously), uses socially constructed categories that inevitably do form the basis of social identities, the second school of thought aims to eliminate any kind of ethnicized or racialized term at the expense of neglecting and obscuring Roma identity and its interplay with structural racism.

In the midst of our current ecological, economic, social and political upheaval, which can be understood as a crisis of neoliberal capitalism or 'precarity capitalism' (Azmanova, 2020), Romani people have become (re-)politicized and (re-)instrumentalized through the constructions of 'Gypsies'/ 'Gypsy criminality' and the 'Gypsy menace'. This has eerie parallels to 20th-century Europe, during the rise of eugenics and Nazi 'race science', which led to the genocidal murders and traumatization of Romani communities across the continent, culminating in the Holocaust (Friedlander, 1995). In this sharp escalation of the racialization of Roma, a majority of progressive scholars have been unable to articulate the centrality of race/racialization in the production of structural violence in neoliberal economies. Furthermore, they have often reinforced the 'colour-blind'/universalist ideologies that masked the enduring structural racism and violence against Roma. All too often in research studies, racism is interpreted in a very narrow sense as an individual moral wrongdoing – as opposed to being structural in nature – that is generally committed by racist, extreme right-wing people. So, the lack of a sociological imagination à la C. Wright Mills, conceptualized as 'the vivid awareness of the relationship between experience and the wider society' (Mills, 1959: 5), contributed (perhaps unwittingly) to *the invisible-izing and silencing of racialization* that became a powerful weapon in the hands of ethno-nationalists and the extreme right, who tacitly instrumentalized anti-Romani racism to enhance the structurally embedded neoliberal racial order. Building upon the path-breaking work of Black scholars, such as Oliver Cox, Cedric J. Robinson and others, who critiqued Marxism for failing to account for the racial character of capitalism (Kelley, 2017), it is suggested that neoliberal racial capitalism gradually unfolded in East Central Europe and South-Eastern Europe after 1989, imposing a systemic condition of crisis that rendered and normalized the vast majority of disenfranchised Roma as 'subhuman' and 'non-human' (Kóczé, forthcoming). Moreover, the structural conditions of neoliberal capitalism forced them to live on the edge of societies, where social, material and environmental destruction escalated (Kóczé and van Baar, 2020).

Arguably, these violent epistemological, knowledge-making legacies led to the subaltern, racialized position that Roma occupy even to this day, a position that leaves Romani communities particularly vulnerable and emanates from the belief that we (the Roma) cede to the non-problematized 'epistemic authority' and uncritically accept whatever is being done for our 'safety' or well-being. Despite the emergence of a tiny group of Romani intellectuals who had achieved some standing, particularly in post-socialist countries, through education from the 1950s onwards, many among them continued to be denigrated, infantilized and marginalized as a result of structural racism underpinned by epistemic violence, that is, *violence rooted at the source of knowledge production on Roma* (Spivak, 1988). Indeed, as Trehan and Matache emphasize in Chapter Seven of this volume, the formal adoption of civil and political rights that promote legal equality does not necessarily ameliorate structures of embedded social and economic oppression.

A Romani feminist perspective: the premise and promise of entering together

It is never just about racism, classism or sexism; it is always the combination of several oppressions that create intersectional obstacles for Romani women. Intersectionality is an analytical concept introduced by Black feminists in the US in the 1970–80s and applied and conceptualized in East Central Europe by contemporary Romani feminists to address the complex reality of Romani women (Kóczé, 2009). In this way, Romani women are similar to other racialized groups whose complex problems are not captured by single-issue social movements. Each of these movements elevated one category and eliminated others. For instance, the Romani rights movement takes up the issue of ethnicity/identity of Roma, women's or feminist movements focus on the issue of gender, the LGBTQI movement focuses on sexuality, and union movements emphasize class. Since Romani women are simultaneously racialized (dehumanized and inferiorized) as Roma, female (with a particular sexual identity) and also as workers (usually underemployed and/ or unemployed), the singular focus on inequality does not therefore capture the complex, lived, racialized social reality.

Intersectionality emerged as an analytical tool to explain these multifaceted challenges faced by Romani women. Confronting multiple forms of discrimination rooted in gendered and racialized power, *both within the community internally and at the societal level*, often leads us to suspend our rights in the name of an illusory 'scientific objectivity' as victimized, racialized and passive female bodies who are de-authorized to produce knowledge. By employing intersectionality as an alternative explanation, Romani feminist scholars transcended the limitations of existing scholarship, using a conceptual language to reveal the racialized, classed and gendered intersected oppressions of Roma at the structural, discursive and biographical levels (Kóczé et al, 2018).

Furthermore, we offer the following critiques and insights:

- We need to understand why existing theoretical frameworks do not explain the actual lived experiences of a majority of Romani women (and men), which are produced by the structures of neoliberal racial capitalism. The 'lived experiences' of Roma must be connected to the structures of the broader political economy.

- Too often, Romani people still feature as informants, ethnographic spectacles, NGO experts (instead of scholars) or activist-scholars whose work is not recognized as an important contribution in its own right. The way forward is to critically reflect on the hierarchical nature of academic knowledge production, as we have begun to do at the Central European University Romani studies programme. This uneasy process entails critical dialogue among Romani and non-Romani scholars, activist-scholars, activists, policymakers and those who implement policies, as well as those who have opportunities to create new knowledge-making avenues and horizons that were hitherto structurally and epistemologically denied to Roma (Kóczé, 2018; Trehan, 2018).

- Ultimately, disruptive epistemological inquiries lead us to diverse perspectives on Romani identity and culture, and Romani life worlds, with the promise of the creation of knowledge that liberates, emancipates and acts as a counter to epistemic violence. There is an urgent need to 'decolonize' Romani studies, as well as to challenge the structural conditions of intersectional racism and sexism, which constantly (re)produce and perpetuate existing racial and gender hierarchies and inequalities. As Yarimar Bonilla, a scholar of post-colonial Caribbean anthropology urges, 'we need to decolonize decolonization … because clearly the formulas that exist today … have only served to reproduce the inequalities of empire' (quoted in Jobson, 2020).

- One of the central critiques raised by Romani feminist scholars is about the non-Romani male domination of the genealogy of knowledge production (Brooks, 2012).

- An 'engaged anthropology' encourages meaningful collaboration with the people who are the objects of study in order to generate social change that seeks to combat the mechanisms of oppressive hierarchization (Beck and

Maida, 2013). Feminist intersectional research aims to be non-hierarchical; however, in academic research protocols, there continue to be hierarchical dimensions nonetheless.

- Instead of exposing the racialization of Roma and the mechanism(s) of structural racism, 'segregationists' and 'assimilationists', per Ibram X. Kendi, attribute the oppression of Roma to their culture (see Chapter Seven by Trehan and Matache). This continues to have a corrosive effect on contemporary structures of thought, crucially, even among some Roma, who have internalized these representations (Acton, 2016).

- Focusing only on Romani culture and marginality, or internal dynamics, without an understanding of the broader processes of capitalist violent race-making and 'othering' in various spheres of society, conceals the scales and manifestations of racial discourses and practices, and hides or disguises the racialized and gendered forces of hierarchical domination in European societies. The gendered racialization of Roma is a process of 'othering' that has profoundly shaped and continues to shape the history, politics, economic structure and culture of European societies.

- The current 'colour-blind' and constructivist sociological approach that is centred around class at the expense of gendered racialization in European academic discourse camouflages the structural racial and gender violence against Roma embedded in a hidden 'racial contract'.

- Emerging critical Romani studies, as envisioned by a fragile minority of Romani and non-Romani scholars, must critique discourses that privilege culturally loaded ethnicity as the only or primary paradigm that frames Romani lived social experiences today.

- In contrast, *epistemic privilege* is socially more complex and tied to opportunities that are structured by gender, race, class, sexuality, citizenship, social networks – even institutional belonging – and so forth. What we mean by this concept is the privilege of those who produce knowledge and who are assumed to have the right to do so. In other words, no one questions a white male in their production of knowledge today (even on Roma), but if a Romani woman is engaged in this task, then she has to prove her 'worth'.

- A significant number of Romani activist-scholars and intellectuals from Central and South-Eastern Europe, who do not circulate in the 'Anglosphere', have limited access to English-language resources, funds and scholarships for higher education, and when their work is published, it often remains marginal or invisible (see Oprea, 2006).

- Activist scholarship provides us with a unique opportunity to learn from errors and to recognize the highly contextual, political and conditional nature of knowledge production within social science, as well as challenge the commodification and marketization of higher education (Ryder, 2018).

Yes, we scholars and activists engaged with Romani life worlds and producing literature in this discipline know that anti-Romani racism has dangerous consequences for the social fabric of Europe, *but to what extent is our knowledge production, our epistemological enterprise, challenging the ideology, conditions and structures that do not validate the knowledge of the racialized community?* As conducting research in this field has political ramifications – and scholars in socialist countries during the time of Soviet hegemony were certainly aware of this – it requires sensitivity to the ethical and political dimensions of knowledge creation on Romani life worlds (Kovats, 2001).

Romani studies scholars must tackle a number of epistemological dilemmas if the goal is to contribute to scholarship that would both challenge and overcome the inherent disciplinary 'silos' of the ivory tower and the hegemonic bias(es) of the status quo, including the gaze of the intrepid, but often myopic, 'gatekeepers' of the field (scholars who define the boundaries of the discipline). One of the most pernicious outcomes of gatekeeping, which runs counter to the spirit of free inquiry and healthy academic debates within the field, continues to be silencing. Voices, insights and constructive criticism deemed to be less valuable are muzzled (And scholars who are women of colour are intimately aware of this!); often, it is the silencing of ideas and philosophies that run counter to the dominant ideology of the day. In her classic piece 'Marginality as a site of resistance', American activist and feminist author bell hooks (1990: 341–3) reminds us of the position of the subaltern, who is almost always objectified by the gatekeeper-cum-colonizer:

> [There is] no need to hear your voice, when I can talk about you better than you can speak about yourself. No need to hear your voice. Only tell me about your pain. I want to know your story. And then I will tell it back to you in a new way. Tell it back to you in such a way that it has become mine, my own.... I am still [the] colonizer, the speaking subject, and you are now at the center of my talk.

Europa, carpe diem! Romani feminism, a New Social Europe and justice for Roma

In this troubled neoliberal capitalist era, we cannot postpone the recognition of the chronic racialized and gendered dispossession of Roma, which – generationally and even to this day – has taken a huge material and emotional toll on those who are living in the midst of a devastating situation. Europe must allocate resources to compensate for the historical injustices of Roma! Europe must change the perverse, competitive distribution of public goods that benefits and rewards those who are structurally well positioned and further disadvantages the most marginalized.

This piece offered a critical theoretical contribution that re-imagines a radically transformed Social Europe by using the language and insights of Romani feminists who challenge the intersected gendered, racial and classed violence not as merely coincidental, *but rather as a systemic condition of neoliberal racial capitalism* (Kóczé, forthcoming) If we want to re-envision Europe, neither the feminist nor the anti-racist Romani movements can afford to ignore the intersectional lived experiences of the vast majority of Romani women who are in a continuous life-and-death struggle for survival and emancipation (Vincze, 2014). Following Kimberlé Crenshaw's (1989) insights, we must centre our intersectional 'politics of re-envisioning' on those who are in the most disadvantaged situation. The reason is that if we start to develop a language/ politics that resonates with the situation of the lived experiences of the most disadvantaged among us, then this will provide the critical basis for solidarity and collective action across European society. As Crenshaw (1989: 167) explains, the goal is to 'facilitate the inclusion of [the most] marginalized groups for whom it can be said: "When they enter, we all enter."' The current political landscape in Europe is replete with political minefields and traps, offering rather illusory notions of inclusion and ambiguous answers to overcome the social exclusion of Roma.

We want to denounce all manifestations of historically accumulated structural, racialized and gendered justice that are not accounted for in the (current) plethora of technical, depoliticized policy recommendations and project-based, piecemeal solutions offered by the European Union and its member states (see Chapter Two). We want to reclaim our epistemic authority, our critical analysis and our theorization (based on the lived experiences, the situation on the ground, at the root level) in order to sharpen the vision of systemic racialized and gendered decay in Europe.

In this critical chapter, we have discussed how epistemic violence continues to reinforce the structural oppression of Roma, and we have suggested ways in which the deep-seated problems of epistemic violence and injustice vis-à-vis Roma can be disrupted by an emerging body of critical Romani scholarship, which would become the basis for a radical redressal of one of Europe's most pernicious wrongs. Indeed, there is now a nucleus of such scholars at the CEU in Budapest/Vienna and at Harvard University's FXB Center for Health and Human Rights, as well as in other institutions and platforms across the globe (museums such as the one in Brno in the Czech Republic, cultural centres such as European Roma Institute for Arts and Culture [ERIAC] in Berlin, RomArchives and so forth).

Black feminist epistemologies also offer us a pathway towards achieving emancipatory knowledge (Collins, 2006). As mentioned earlier and in Chapter Seven by Trehan and Matache, the strong parallels between Romani and African-American experiences of oppression are undeniable, and the quest for justice for Roma has been deeply influenced by the work of US civil rights leaders, from Ida B. Wells, to Martin Luther King Jr, to the Black Lives Matter movement of today.

Inspired by the poignant article of civil rights lawyer and legal scholar Michelle Alexander (2020), 'America this is your chance', after the brutal murder of George Floyd forced the US to embark upon a national reckoning, we too exhort Europe to seize the day and face courageously its racial history and racial present. European public intellectuals and politicians continue to deny and/or underplay the depth of anti-Romani racism embedded within their societies. That is why we welcome the report of the EU's Fundamental Rights Agency (FRA), 'A persisting concern', officially recognizing, for the first time, that 'anti-Gypsyism … [is] a key *structural* driver of Roma exclusion that undermines the *process* intended to decrease Roma deprivation' (FRA, 2018: 8, emphases original). As Director of the FRA Michael O'Flaherty emphasizes:

the Roma population continue to struggle with challenges we like to believe no longer exist in the EU. Homes without running water or electricity, lack of health insurance, and even hunger continue to be realities for unacceptable shares of the Roma community in one of the richest regions in the world. (FRA, 2018: 3)

Acknowledging that anti-Romani racism underpins Romani exclusion is the first step in initiating systemic transformation to rectify structural violence in Europe. Indeed, racial profiling, police abuse and violence, and the disproportionate incarceration of Roma are only the tip of the iceberg; all require urgent redressal by EU institutions and member states so that the long-awaited promise of justice for Roma is ultimately achieved.

References

Acton, T. (2016) 'Scientific racism, popular racism and the discourse of the Gypsy Lore Society', *Ethnic and Racial Studies*, 39(7): 1187–204.

Alexander, M. (2020) 'America this is your chance', *The New York Times*, 8 June.

Azmanova, A. (2020) *Capitalism on Edge: How Fighting Precarity Can Achieve Radical Change Without Crisis or Utopia*, New York: Columbia University Press.

Beck, S. and Maida, C. (eds) (2013) *Toward Engaged Anthropology*, New York, NY: Berghahn.

Brooks, E. (2012) 'The possibilities of Romani feminism', *Signs*, 38(1): 111.

Collins, P.H. (2006) 'Patricia Hill Collins: Intersecting oppressions', www.semanticscholar.org/paper/Patricia-Hill-Collins-%3A-Intersecting-Oppressions-Collins/a976d21759a3647422ea3025 2a1997aab5c6cbd5

Crenshaw, K. (1989) 'Demarginalizing the intersection of race and sex: A black feminist critique of antidiscrimination doctrine, feminist theory and antiracist politics', *University of Chicago Legal Forum*, 1: 1–31.

FRA (Fundamental Right Agency) (2018) 'A persisting concern: Anti-Gypsyism as a barrier to Roma inclusion', http://fra.europa.eu/en/publication/2018/roma-inclusion

Friedlander, H. (1995) *Origins of Nazi Genocide: From Euthanasia to the Final Solution*, Chapel Hill, NC: University of North Carolina Press.

Galván-Álvarez, E. (2010) 'Violencia y venganza epistemológica: La cuestión de las formas de conocimiento en Mother India' ['Epistemic violence and retaliation: The issue of knowledges in Mother India'], *Atlantis*, 32(2): 11–26.

hooks, b. (1990) 'Marginality as a site of resistance', in R. Ferguson, M. Gever, T. Minh-ha and C. West (eds) *Out There: Marginalization and Contemporary Cultures*, Cambridge, MA: MIT Press, New Museum of Contemporary Art, pp 341–3.

Jobson, R.C. (2020) 'Public thinker: Yarimar Bonilla on decolonizing decolonization', *Public Thinker*, 27 May, www.publicbooks.org/public-thinker-yarimar-bonilla-on-decolonizing-decolonization/

Kelley, R.D.G. (2017) 'What did Cedric Robinson mean by racial capitalism?', *Boston Review*, 12 January.

Kóczé, A. (2018) 'Transgressing borders: Challenging racist and sexist epistemology' in S. Beck and A. Ivasiuc (eds) *Roma Activism: Reimagining Power and Knowledge*, Oxford: Berghahn, pp 111–29.

Kóczé, A. (2020) 'Racialization, racial oppression of Roma', in I. Ness and Z. Cope (eds) *The Palgrave Encyclopedia of Imperialism and Anti-Imperialism*, London: Palgrave Macmillan.

Kóczé, A. (forthcoming) *Gender, Race, and Class: Romani Women's Political Struggle in Post-Socialist Europe*.

Kóczé, A., with Popa, M. (2009) *Missing Intersectionality: Race/Ethnicity, Gender, and Class in Current Research and Policies on Romani Women in Europe*, CEU Working Paper Series, Budapest: Center for Policy Studies, Central European University, www.cps-policy-study-missing-intersectionality-2009.pdf

Kóczé, A. and van Baar, H. (eds) (2020) *The Roma and their Struggle for Identity in Contemporary Europe*, Oxford: Berghahn.

Kóczé, A., Zentai, V., Vince, E. and Jovanovic, J. (eds) (2018) *The Romani Women's Movement: Struggles and Debates in Central and Eastern Europe*, London and New York, NY: Routledge.

Kovats, M. (2001) 'Problems of intellectual and political accountability in respect of emerging European Roma policy', *Journal of Ethnopolitics and Minority Issues in Europe*, 1: 1–9.

Lee, K. (2000) 'Orientalism and Gypsylorism', *Social Analysis: The International Journal of Social and Cultural Practice*, 44(2): 129–56.

Matache, M. (2017) 'Dear Gadje (non-Romani) scholars...', *The Huffington Post* blog, 16 June, https://fxb.harvard.edu/2017/06/19/dear-gadje-non-romani-scholars/

Mills, C.W. (1959) *The Sociological Imagination*, New York, NY: Oxford University Press.

Oprea, A. (2006) 'Re-envisioning social justice from the ground up: Including the experiences of Romani women', *Essex Human Rights Review*, 1(1): 29–39.

Ryder, A. (2018) 'Paradigm shift and Romani studies: Research "on" or "for" and "with" the Roma', in S. Beck and A. Ivasiuc (eds) *Roma Activism: Reimagining Power and Knowledge*, Oxford: Berghahn Books, pp 91–111.

Spivak, G.C. (1988) 'Can the subaltern speak?', in Nelson, C. and Grossberg, L. (eds) *Marxism and the Interpretation of Culture*, Basingstoke: Macmillan, pp 271–313.

Trehan, N. (2009) 'Human rights entrepreneurship in post-Socialist Hungary: From "Gypsy problem" to "Romani rights"', PhD thesis, London School of Economics.

Trehan, N. (2018) 'The epistemological enterprise and the problem of structural violence: Intersectional and interdisciplinary approaches to the production of emancipatory knowledge in Romani studies', paper presented at the 'Critical Approaches to Romani Studies' conference, CEU, 24–25 May, Budapest.

Vincze, E. (2014) 'The racialization of Roma in the "New" Europe and the political potential of Romani women', *European Journal of Women's Studies*, 21(4): 435–42.

Wynter, S. (2003) 'Unsettling the coloniality of being/power/truth/freedom: Towards the human, after man, its overrepresentation. An argument', *The New Centennial Review*, 3(3): 257–337.

Afterword: solidarity and equity in a New Social Europe

Romeo Franz

Europe has over 12 million Roma. About six million of them live in the European Union (EU) and just over three quarters live in extreme poverty. Denying the right to a decent life, for at least 4.5 million EU citizens, is not just a matter of social rights, but also a question of how the EU treats its most important resource – its people. Roma are a young population – indeed, 40 per cent are children and adolescents. If member states can ensure equal access to quality services, including early childhood development and education services, health, housing, and employment, just imagine the positive difference this investment could make! Not only would the Roma improve their lives, but it would also allow them to contribute fully to the future of the EU and the countries in which they live.

In this context, the EU and its member states must be aware, finally, of the potential of the Romani contribution to the future of the European project, to its social and economic development. For example, the good health of the Romani population and access to quality education and infrastructure (clean drinking water, adequate public transport to rural areas and information technology connectivity) are essential preconditions for the full participation of Roma in the social life and labour market of their country. Take the example of

Romani workers in the factories and farms of many Western European countries. They are playing a key role in supporting the economies of these counties, even if for many of them the working conditions are not so friendly. Sometimes, their salaries are not, at all, expressing the value of the amount of work they do every single day. They live in overcrowded rented houses, two or three families, with children, struggling in a foreign country for a better life. They are not so visible, but they are some of the heroes of our day.

To make the equal treatment of Romani people a reality, there is a strong need for a post-2020 EU Strategic Framework for the Equality, Inclusion and Participation of people with Romani background, with a binding character for the member states in terms of Romani inclusion goals to be reached. Political support when racism against different minority groups is rising sharply is a key point for the inclusion of Romani people. Major mobilization of key stakeholders in exploring the opportunities around the upcoming EU presidencies is needed to ensure political commitment for a post-2020 potential binding policy. Following this approach, adequate funding would be allocated and it could lead to a more successful implementation of the national strategies or action plans, especially at regional and local levels. The EU must link its political and financial priorities to priorities regarding the inclusion of people with Romani background. When local and national budgets are developed, the inclusion of people with Romani background will be among the priorities. More efficient and strengthened monitoring and oversight mechanisms must be developed, and the European Commission and member states must ensure that the funds allocated are properly spent and not misused if the strategic framework is to deliver on its goals.

To achieve this in an effective way, the European Commission and the member states must move from the paternalistic (top to bottom) approach mainly used for the development of the current framework, to the non-paternalistic one. A bottom-up approach would allow people with Romani background to participate more effectively in policymaking at all levels; local and regional stakeholders (non-governmental organizations, activists, experts, community members and so on) must also be involved in the development, implementation and monitoring of the post-2020 public policies towards people with Romani background. Considering the non-paternalistic approach, the post-2020 EU Strategic Framework for the Equality, Inclusion and Participation of people with Romani background could be developed based on more reliable quantitative and qualitative data; future strategies would be based on the latest available information since access to a larger number of communities and considerable sources of solutions for the improvement of the Romani situation would be broader than in 2011. These data must be the basis of detailed and realistic action plans, with a realistic and adequate predefined budget included into the national, regional and local budgets according to the magnitude of the social inclusion needs of people with Romani background.

However, COVID-19 has shown, very clearly, the failure of the governments within the EU to treat Romani people as equal citizens. It has shown that persistent and structural antigypsyism continues to exist at all levels of European society, and manifests itself on a daily basis.

Under lockdowns, many Romani people suffer disproportionately. Besides the lack of access to potable drinking water, food or sanitation equipment to keep them safe from infection, Romani men, women and children were brutally beaten and abused by police forces, especially in Eastern European countries, such as Romania, Bulgaria and Slovakia. Moreover, they also became the targets of xenophobic rumours and conspiracies in countries such as Spain, singling them out as the transmitters of the COVID-19 virus.

Racism is not the 'solution' to this crisis; we need to be supportive. The virus does not care about wealth, poverty or ethnicity; it can hit everyone. When it does, if we do not make sure we protect the most vulnerable among us, it can be lethal, not just for those infected, but for an entire community.

This is why the EU and its member states cannot afford to lose more time and play with human lives by legitimizing the work on the inclusion of people with Romani background through a soft policy like the 2011–20 EU Roma Framework. Member states must officially recognize antigypsyism as a specific form of racism against people with a Romani background, and to develop and implement specific and effective preventive and corrective measures against it on all levels where it occurs.

Unfortunately, antigypsyism is one of the oldest forms of racism in European history, from the time of slavery in Romania to the Holocaust and present day. The majority societies must know our history, and our traditions and culture, before judging us. We have been citizens of our countries for centuries. Many of our people fought in wars and defended the integrity of our countries, while many were murdered during the Holocaust because of their ethnicity. Yet, this part of our history and our contribution to our countries' development is not properly acknowledged in school curricula. We need to raise awareness about this, and the EU and its member states can play an important role in this matter.

Antigypsyism has kept Roma in deep poverty. Today, this is still a taboo subject for the EU and many European countries. Antigypsyism is one of the main obstacles for equal participation and inclusion of people with a Romani background. Without a horizontal approach against antigypsyism in all domains of public life, we cannot speak about a real change and successful inclusion process.

This is why we need to urgently call on the European Commission to develop a proposal for a post-2020 EU Strategic Framework for Equality, Inclusion and Participation of people with Romani background in Europe, putting the fight against poverty and antigypsyism at the forefront. The proposal must include: clear and binding objectives, measures and targets for the member states; a clear timeline and clear and binding progress requirements, as well as success indicators and adequate funding for its implementation; and a robust monitoring and oversight mechanism to ensure effective implementation and appropriate use of funds. Equal participation in all domains of public life, political participation and the language, arts, culture, history and environmental injustice of people with Romani background should be explicitly mentioned in the proposal for a post-2020 EU public policy, with additional measures to the four main priority areas of education, employment, housing and healthcare.

However, this cannot be done in solitude. It requires a joint effort of people with a Romani background across Europe. The power of numbers speaking with the same voice towards the achievement of a common goal must be a priority of our communities and its leadership – *Opre Roma* (Roma Arise)!

Index